AN INTRODUCTION TO
CALLIGRAPHY

RUFUS

RUFUS.

AN INTRODUCTION TO
CALLIGRAPHY

GEORGE EVANS

THE
APPLE
PRESS

For Inge and George, in appreciation of their support over the years and Christine for her assistance in compiling the book.

A QUINTET BOOK

Published by Apple Press Ltd.
6 Blundell Street
London N7 9BH

ISBN 1-85076-100-0

Reprinted 1989

This book was designed and produced by Quintet Publishing Limited

Designer: George Evans
Research: Christine Cash
Editors: Robert Stewart, Shaun Barrington
Photographer: Paul Forrester
All calligraphy by George Evans

Extracts from *The Hobbit* by Professor J R R Tolkien courtesy of Unwin Hyman Ltd, UK, and Houghton Mifflin Publishers, US.

Typeset in Great Britain by
Central Southern Typesetters, Eastbourne, in Linotron Plantin
Headings in Asmyth Light

Manufactured in Hong Kong by Regent Publishing Services Limited
Printed in Hong Kong by South Sea Int'l Press Ltd.

The author and producers of this book would like to thank Osmiroid (E.S. Perry), Graphikos Design, Langford and Hill Ltd, and especially Falkiner Fine Papers Ltd of Covent Garden, London, for the use of their materials and equipment.

CONTENTS

Ein bißchen mehr Freude und weniger Streit;

Ein bißchen mehr Güte und weniger Neid;

Ein bißchen mehr Wahrheit immerdar—;

Und viel mehr Hilfe bei Gefahr—;

Ein bißchen mehr Kraft—nicht so zimperlich;

Ein bißchen mehr Wir und weniger Ich;

Und viel mehr Blumen während des Lebens;

Denn auf den Gräbern blüh'n sie vergebens.

(CALLIGRAPHY by George Evans 1966)

INTRODUCTION

Sans
Serifed
Italic
Gothic
UNCIA

Five different lettering styles to be found in this book.

Few people who pick up a calligraphic pen for the first time ever produce a masterpiece. Many are so disappointed with the results that they give up. After all, lettering and calligraphy would appear to be just an extension of handwriting, taught in school. This is far from the truth. Dedication and an appreciation of letterforms and space are essential in this most disciplined of arts.

After leaving school, I was fortunate to be given the opportunity to study graphic design. After only one lesson of tracing letterforms from a printer's specimen sheet, I realized that lettering was by far the most exciting part of the design course. Within a few weeks I was lettering with a brush and pointed pen. It was a further six months before I tried a square-ended nib and calligraphy.

The first serious piece of work I produced was lettered for my grandmother in 1966. I actually spent two weekends before a sheet came off the drawing board which I felt was worth posting to her. It has, however, survived 21 years. At that time, I was not aware of calligraphic styles; so I based the letterforms on a name seen on a perfume bottle. Since then my relationship with and understanding of letterforms has grown stronger.

The work and alphabets included in this book have been reproduced, wherever possible, in their original lettered size, without retouching for the printing process. I hope that this approach will help when studying and assist by giving an honest comparison when checking progress.

Although each letter in an alphabet has its own trait, there are elements that are common to each letter, giving uniformity and continuity to the lettering. It is therefore necessary to become aware of the main characteristics of any given style before lettering is commenced. Examine the round letters; they will all have similarities in weight of stroke and curvature. Likewise a pattern will emerge when comparing both the straight and oblique strokes. The alphabet as a whole should appear as one, without anomalies and in complete harmony.

This book aims to assist the student to become proficient with a pen. More than that, it invites him or her to become aware of the letterforms which surround us all. I firmly believe that speed and ease of learning are of the essence and, providing willingness is there on the student's part, together with patience — as a fair amount of this virtue will be needed – by the end of this book he or she should be well on their way to enjoying the pleasures of lettering.

Over a period of time, the student will develop a warm, personal relationship with letterforms and will become familiar with the individual characteristics of letterforms within the numerous alphabet styles which exist. He may even advance to the point of developing a new style of his own.

Once the inhibitions of committing pen to paper are overcome and confidence starts running, most students wonder how they ever lived without letterforms.

The first piece of calligraphy I produced, in 1966.

7

WHAT IS CALLIGRAPHY?

In order to understand and participate in the subject, the word calligraphy must be defined. The dictionary states 'handwriting or penmanship', or simply 'beautiful handwriting'. My own definition is much tighter and reads 'letters produced by the means of a square-ended implement'. This includes quill pens, reed pens, metal pens, brushes, felt- or fibre-tip pens and even a piece of card or wood – in fact, anything with a square end capable of producing an image on a variety of surfaces by leaving an ink or medium deposit.

The earliest evidence of a written hand is a limestone tablet of around 3500 BC, which is made up from pictograms. These developed into ideograms – pictures to represent ideas or less definite objects. Finally phonograms were used – these were symbols representing sounds.

However, the roots of our present-day letters are to be found in the Roman alphabet of the first century AD. These majuscule, or capital, letters were mainly for incising into stone with a chisel and I believe that they owe their shape to this fact. The best-known surviving example of Quadrata, or Square Capital, lettering is an inscription to be found at the foot of Emperor Trajan's Column in Rome, AD 114. This fine, chiselled lettering is held to be a model for all artists to follow. It has certainly stood the test of time, although there is some conjecture as to the production of this work. It has been suggested that the letters were formed initially by a lettering artist with a brush and then cut by a stone craftsman. The style of the lettering, however, reflects more the action of the chisel than that of the brush, especially when considering the fine serifs, which form the ends of the main strokes of the letters. In order to cut lettering into stone, the V-groove chisel starts at the surface and cuts into the material to form the deeper channel of the main stroke. It would almost appear that the serifs (letter beginnings and endings) became an essential part of the process, later being squared off to form a cap and foot to the letter.

The Romans used a second main style called Rustica. This was a less formal, more fluid, letterform than Quadrata and was principally produced with a pen or a brush. It is more elongated than Quadrata, and this, coupled with its flowing form, made it an economical style to use in books as more writing could be contained within a page. There were other decorative Roman styles but they have little relevance in this book.

Calligraphers and letter designers are still emulating the incised square capital. Much of this can be ascribed to the evolution from one style to another and much to tradition. However, the very shape of a square-ended implement utilized in producing letterforms naturally dictates its own starting and ending points, thus negating the need for an additional serif, which must be regarded as adornment only. Many styles said to have evolved through a desire for speed are unbelievably elaborate for their intended purpose. If speed were of the essence, surely the fewer the strokes, the more efficient the style. It must therefore be accepted that calligraphic forms are rarely written for ease and with communication as the prime factor: more often than not, artistic appearance is given priority over legibility.

This book reflects both traditional and modern styles, but with the emphasis on legibility and practical usage when compiling alphabet samples.

An example of the informal style, 'Rustica.'

Modern incised lettering.

NOMENCLATURE

In order to discuss the subject of letters, calligraphers, letter designers and students require terminology to describe the constituent parts of letterforms. When analyzing a particular style, this nomenclature is used to define the various elements in a concise manner. There is no standard nomenclature to define constituent parts of letters but many of the terms are self-explanatory. The terminology used here is based on that employed by letter designers and therefore may differ from that found in calligraphic references. Many descriptions are repeated from letter to letter as these terms are used generally throughout the alphabet and are not necessarily confined to a specific letter. The parts and names illustrated refer to the Quadrata capitals (majuscule) and a complementary lower-case (minuscule) alphabet although most of the terms can be employed to define other forms.

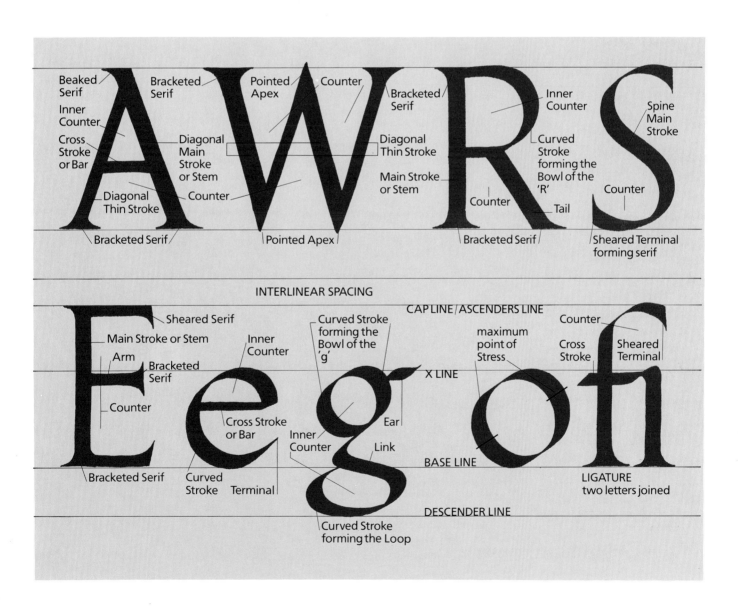

ROMAN CLASSICAL ALPHABET

ABC
DEFGHIJKLM
NOPQRSTU
VWXYZ
&1234567890
abcdefghijklm
nopqrstuvw
xyz

UNDERSTANDING LETTER CONSTRUCTION

Quadrata is the criterion on which all subsequent styles are based. It is therefore of prime importance for students to associate themselves with this fine, proportioned alphabet.

Roman is not just the name of the country of origin but is used more generally to describe any style appearing in a vertical attitude. The capital alphabet contains more straight lines than curves, and many letters have a combination of both vertical and horizontal strokes giving a squarish appearance, hence the word Quadrata. There is an architectural, geometric quality within the style which would account for the harmony created when lettering is used on buildings in stone.

Capital letters can be defined as having a uniform height throughout; that is, they are written between two parallel lines. The letters are contained within a capital line (top line) and a base line, with the exception of the letters 'J' and 'Q' which break the base line in some styles. The lines are also marginally broken by minor optical adjustments to certain letters where pointed apexes and curved strokes slightly overlap.

There are now two fixed points, the capital and the base lines, between which to construct the letters. There is, however, a problem. It must be decided how far apart the lines should be drawn. Consider the proportions of the letters opposite. There is a definite relationship between the capital height and the width of the main stroke. In Quadrata the stem divides into the capital height 10 times, giving a ratio of 1:10. It is important to evaluate this ratio, as misinterpretation will result in an untrue reproduction of the style.

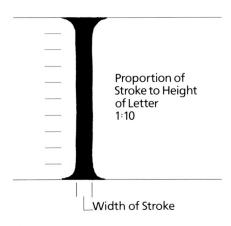

Proportion of
Stroke to Height
of Letter
1:10

Width of Stroke

Once the height and weight ratios have been established, consideration must be given to the construction of individual letters. The Romans were a practical and efficient race, and their ability to rationalize and organize is reflected in the formal appearance of their design. The alphabet which follows has been produced with a pen and is based on formal Roman characters. If the forms are analyzed, it will be noticed that there are similar characteristics between certain letters, the 'E', 'F' and 'L' for example.

It is also apparent that the widths of letters are not identical and that each character occupies a given area in width while retaining a constant height. This width is known as the unit value of the letter, the 'M' and 'W' being the widest and the 'I' and 'J' the narrowest. The unit width is a necessary factor in determining the final balance and poise of letters.

When letters are placed on a gridded square, an immediate visual comparison between the letterforms is possible. The grid illustrated has been divided into units of stem width for convenience, giving an initial square for the capitals subdivided into 10 units of height by 10 units of width. The lower blank portion is for the lower case letters, which appear after the capitals. The lower portion will then be used to accommodate the descenders of the lower case.

Incidentally, the words 'lower case' are a printers' term, now in common use to describe minuscule letters. It derives from the typesetters' cases which contained the metal or wooden letters. The capital letters of an alphabet were stored in the upper case and so are sometimes referred to as such, with the small letters stored in the lower case.

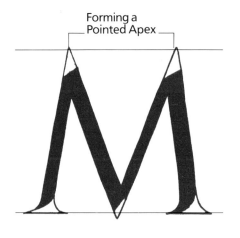

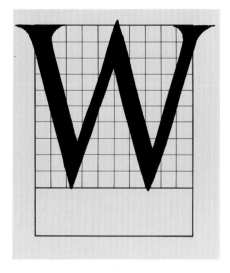

Forming a Pointed Apex

Although concerned with calligraphy here, I feel that the common terms for majuscule and minuscule letters – capitals and lower case – are better employed and I will use this terminology from now onwards.

When analyzing the construction of individual characters, it is essential for the student to fix their images firmly in his mind. The proportions of this style will be found to be indispensable as the student becomes more involved with letterforms, and the ability to draw on his experience of the classical Roman style will assist him when analyzing other letterforms. The letters fall into six groupings, from the widest to the narrowest characters.

I have lettered this alphabet with a pen to illustrate proportion; it also shows that a classical Roman style can be achieved calligraphically. It is not my intention that the student begins lettering with this style. The construction of the letterforms is difficult in as much as they are not easily reproduced with a square-ended nib. Within the sample alphabet sheets there is a Roman style that has been simplified for use with the pen. Even so it will be seen that it is deliberately the last alphabet entry and therefore requires a degree of penmanship.

ROMAN CAPITALS

Group 1
The 'M' is one of the widest letters of the alphabet, occupying slightly more than the square with the diagnoal strokes breaking the grid at both sides. The true Roman 'M' has pointed apexes, along with the 'A' and 'N', which are easily cut with a chisel; but when a pen or brush is employed, other forms of ending the strokes are more natural.

In order to achieve a pointed apex the pen strokes end short of the cap and base lines and are then brought to a point. The apexes project beyond capital and base lines in order to obtain optical alignment with letters ending in square terminals or with beaked or bracketed serifs. Because the apexes of the 'M' in the example alphabet end in a beaked serif, this will naturally be carried through to the 'A' and 'N' to give continuity. The straight, thin strokes in the 'M' and similar letters are approximately half the thickness of the main stroke, but these strokes do alter because of the fixed lettering angle of the pen in relation to the direction of the strokes.

The 'W' is perhaps the widest letter of the alphabet. It does not appear in Roman inscriptions but is a medieval addition to the alphabet. In Latin inscriptions 'V' stood for both the 'U' and 'V' sounds – hence the name 'double U', drawn as two 'V's virtually joined together, with minor adjustments. The 'U' symbol was a later development, perhaps to avoid confusion.

Group 2
The 'O' sets the standard for all curved letters and the 'Q' can be said to be an 'O' with an added tail. It is advisable to make note of the point at which the tail joins the curved stroke. Some letters, unfortunately, have a tail which appears to emanate from the lower left-hand curve of the letter, as

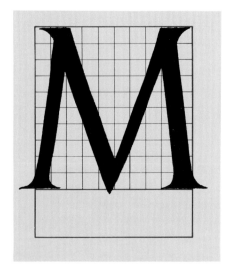

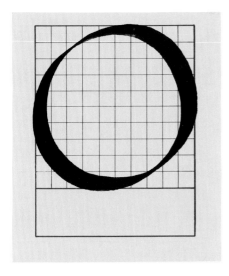

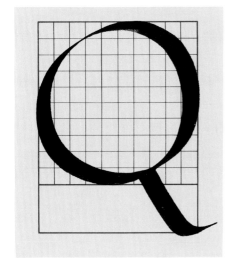

an extension. This, in my view, is undesirable as the tail is most definitely a separate stroke.

The widest point of the thick stroke of the 'O' is marginally wider than that of the stem of the 'I'. In a free-drawn letter, that is a letter drawn and then filled in, this is an optical adjustment made to compensate for the tapering or thinning of the stroke towards the thinnest part of the letter. Without this alteration the curved stroke would appear optically thinner than the stem of the 'I'.

In calligraphy, the adjustment to thicken the curved strokes is automatic because of the oblique angle of the pen to the direction of writing. The thin strokes are substantially thinner than half the width of the main stroke, due to this same action of the pen. If desired, these thin strokes can be thickened to compare more favourably with the straight thin strokes. I have not done so, because I feel the characters should reflect the nature of the tool.

The widest point of the curved stroke is known as the 'maximum point of stress' and in this example it can be said that the letter has diagonal stress with oblique shading. There are many styles which have horizontal stress with vertical shading.

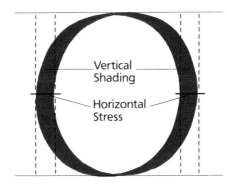
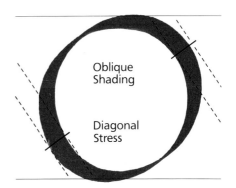

Group 3

The 'C', 'D' and 'G' take up about nine-tenths of the width of the gridded square. Because they are all rounded forms, the top and bottom curves project slightly over the cap and base lines. This is to ensure that the round letters appear the same height as those ending in flat serifs. Without this refinement they would appear smaller.

The 'C' follows the left-hand curve of the 'O', but the upper and lower arms are somewhat flattened. The upper arm ends in a sheared terminal which is slightly extended to form a beak-like serif. In Quadrata the lower arm also ends similarly. This serif is extremely difficult to produce with a pen.

'G' follows the lines of the 'C', with the stem of the 'G' rising from the lower arm to within five-tenths of the letter height and terminating in a bracketed serif. I prefer the stem slightly shorter at four-tenths.

'D' follows the right-hand curve of the 'O' with the upper and lower curves extending from the initial cross-strokes, so slightly breaking the cap line and base line. The stem appears slightly thickened towards the base cross-stroke where it is joined with a curved bracket. The serifs are bracketed on the left hand of the stem.

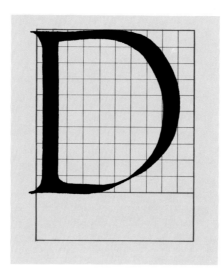
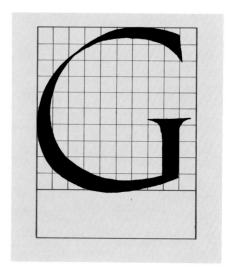

Group 4

This is the largest group of letters and includes 'A', 'H', 'K', 'N', 'R', 'T', 'U', 'V', 'X', 'Y' and 'Z', all of which occupy approximately eight-tenths of the gridded square.

The 'A', 'V', 'X' and 'Y', being letters formed from triangular elements, should appear almost symmetrical. The 'V' and inverted 'V' shapes should be balanced, not leaning to right or left. The cross-stroke of the 'A' is positioned midway between the apex and the base line.

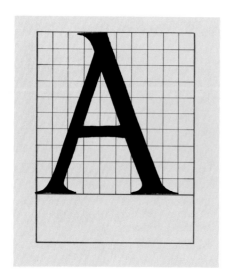
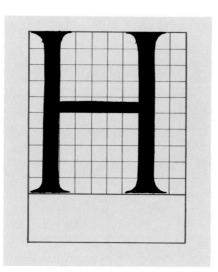
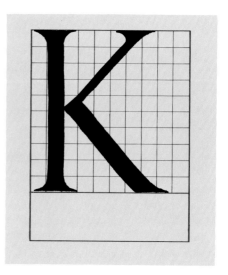

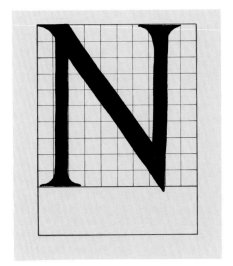

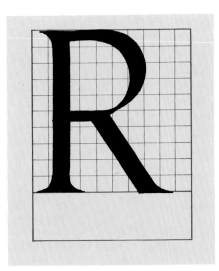

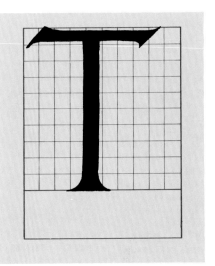

The cross-bar of the 'H' should be slightly above the centre line; otherwise it seems to be slipping down the main stems. The two diagonal strokes of the 'K' meet at a point which, too, is slightly above the centre, making the lower counter fractionally larger than the upper counter.

The pointed apex of the 'N' should protrude below the base line with the upper left-hand serif being beaked. Both the upper part of the bowl of the 'R' and the curved stroke of the 'U' project above the cap line and below the base line respectively. The top of the lower cross-stroke which joins the bowl of the 'R' is positioned on the centre line. A careful note should be made as to where the tail of the 'R' meets the bowl.

The cross-bar of the 'T' is sheared to the lettering angle on the left and right sides, ending in a slight serif. The spurs added to the serifs protrude above the cap line.

The 'Z' is a problem letter as the main diagonal stem requires a change of pen angle to thicken the stroke. Otherwise the stem would appear as a hairline-thin stroke. This makes it difficult to execute with the pen.

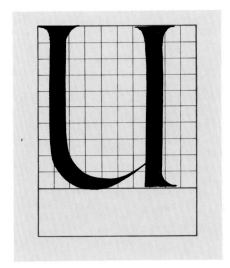

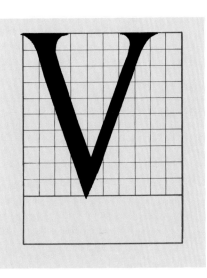

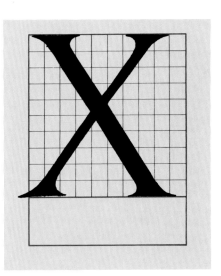

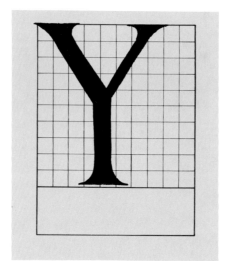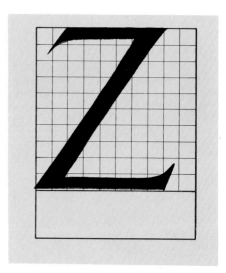

Group 5

Within this group are the letters 'B', 'E', 'F', 'L', 'P' and 'S', each letter occupying about half the width of the gridded square. The upper bowl of the 'B' is smaller than the lower and therefore the intersection is above the centre line. This is intentional: if both bowls were equal in size the letter would appear top-heavy.

The upper arm of the 'E' is slightly longer than the middle arm, which is placed high on the centre line, making the upper counter smaller than the lower. Again this is optically necessary. The lower arm projects a little beyond the upper arm with both ending in sheared, bracketed serifs.

The 'F' may be regarded as an 'E' minus the lower arm. The 'L' is an 'E' without the upper arms. The stem at the cap line has the addition of a bracketed serif on the right.

The letter 'P' at first glance resembles a 'B' minus the lower bowl. Closer inspection will show that the bowl is larger than the upper bowl of

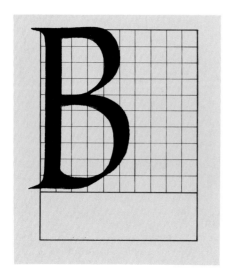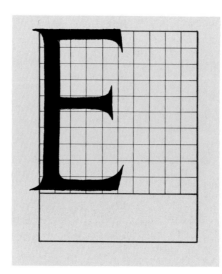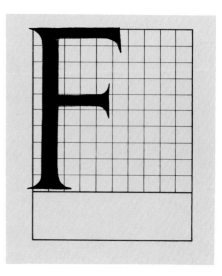

'B'. The cross-stroke joins the bowl to the stem below the centre line.

The upper counter of the 'S' is smaller than the lower counter, with the letter sloping slightly to the right. The diagonal spine is of uniform thickness until it tapers to meet the curved arms. The 'S' is a diagonally stressed letter, having this characteristic in common with the 'A', 'K', 'M', 'N', 'R', 'V', 'W' and, in this alphabet, the 'Z', which is the only letter with a thick diagonal stroke running from top right to bottom left. The upper and lower arms end in sheared terminals and fractionally extend to form beak-like serifs. Being the only letter with diagonal stress it is important for balance that the lower counter is slightly larger than the upper counter. This gives the 'S' a slight forward tilt, making it one of the hardest letters in which to achieve good poise.

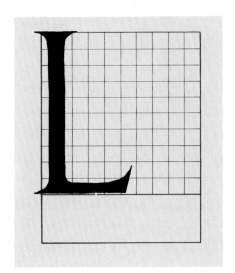

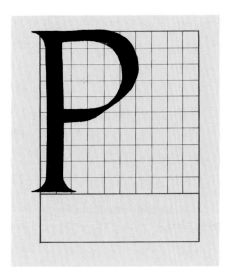

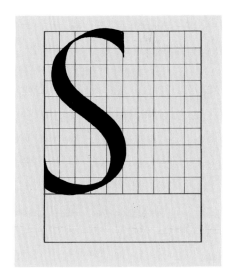

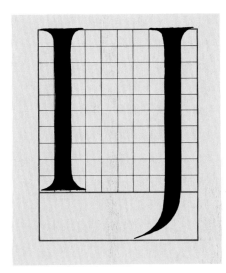

Group 6

The 'I' and 'J' take up approximately three-tenths of the gridded square. The 'I' is a simply constructed letter. Nevertheless, it is important because it sets the standard for the alphabet in height and stem width.

The 'J' does not appear in the inscription on the Trajan Column where its present-day sound is represented by an 'I'. 'J' is written like an 'I' minus the base-line bracketed serif, where the stroke continues through the base line and curves to the left, ending in a pointed terminal. The length of the stroke is contained within the descender area.

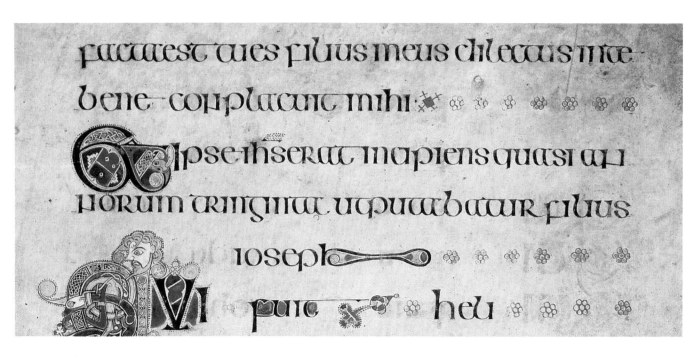

THE DEVELOPMENT OF LOWER CASE (MINUSCULES)

The Quadrata and Rustica capitals were followed by Uncial, born of the need to write more quickly while still maintaining a formal style. Uncial is a true pen form with a simple construction and comparatively clean finishing strokes. Uncial was the literary hand for fine books from the fifth to the eighth century. The letterforms were more rounded than traditional Roman capitals. The chief characteristic letters within the style were the 'A', 'D', 'E', 'H' and 'M' and, although they were still written between the capital and base lines, certain letters, namely the 'D', 'F', 'G', 'H', 'K', 'L', 'P', 'Q', 'X' and 'Y', began to have longer stems which marginally broke through the cap and base lines.

Uncial was followed by Half-Uncial and here some letters are seen predominantly to break through the writing lines forming ascender and descender areas. Letterforms were modified, notably the 'a', 'b', 'e', 'g' and 'l', with the remaining letters receiving only minor amendments, if any at all. Half-Uncial led the way for other minuscule scripts to be developed.

Towards the end of the eighth century, with the revival of learning, came a reform of the hand in which works of literature were to be written. The emperor Charlemagne, who governed a vast area of Europe, commissioned the abbot and teacher, Alcuin of York, to rationalize and standardize the various minuscule scripts which had developed. Alcuin studied the former styles of Quadrata, Rustica, Uncial and Half-Uncial and developed a new minuscule as a standard book style. This has become known as the Carolingian minuscule after its instigator, the emperor Charlemagne. Calligraphy now entered a new era with this distinctive true pen form.

A comparison of the Uncial and Half Uncial letterforms.

An example of Uncial and Half Uncial lettering from the Book of Kells.

Although the Romans used mainly capital letterforms, I have included a classical lower-case alphabet, together with Arabic numerals, to complement the capital forms previously described, and to give the student an insight into their construction. The letters and numerals that follow are of classical proportions and, once their relative widths and construction details have been mastered, knowledge of them will stand the student in good stead for lettering the sample alphabets in this book.

The letters have been placed on a grid which consists of squares of stem width: thirteen units deep, with four units allocated for the ascenders (those letters which reach the cap or ascender line, the 'h' for instance), six units for the x height (that portion of the grid which contains letters such as the 's') and three units below the x height (to accommodate the descenders of letters such as the 'g' and 'y'). I have grouped together the characters with common widths, starting with the widest and ending with the narrowest.

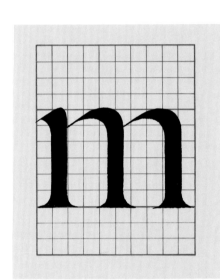

Group 1

The lowercase 'm' and 'w' occupy approximately 10 units, and both letters are contained within the x height. In the 'm', observe the point at which the curved shoulder of the second stroke meets the stem of the first — the second shoulder intersects at the same height. The serif of the first stroke and both shoulders, because they are curved, are positioned so that they break the x line to give optical alignment with the letters 'v', 'w', 'x', 'y' and 'z'; their tops are either bracketed serifs or, in the 'z', a cross-stroke.

The 'm' is not two 'n's joined, as the inner counters of the 'm' are narrower than that of the 'n'. The apexes of the 'w' extend slightly below the base line and the inner apex is the x line. This shows that the diagonal strokes are positioned correctly.

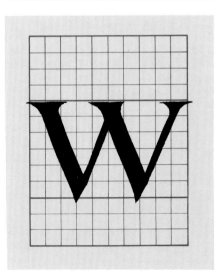

Group 2

Each letter in this group occupies about seven units. The group comprises 'd', 'g', 'h', 'k', 'n', 'p', 'q', 'u', 'x' and 'y'. There are three letters with ascenders ('d', 'h' and 'k'), four letters with descenders ('g', 'p', 'q' and 'y'), and three contained within the x height.

In the 'd', at the point where the lower curve of the bowl meets the main stem, there should be a triangular space formed by the upward movement of the curved stroke. The upper serif of the main stem projects slightly above the ascender or cap line.

The old-style 'g' is very difficult to master. In this style the bowl does not take up the whole depth of the x height: instead it occupies just over three units. It then joins the link which carries down to the base line and then turns sharply to the right and ends forming the right side of the loop. The loop is accommodated within the three-unit descender area. The ear is attached to the bowl at the right side, leaving a v-shaped space.

The 'h' and 'n' are formed in a similar fashion, although the 'h' has the first stem lengthened to form the ascender, with the serif extending over the ascender line. The letter 'n' can be taken as an 'h' without the ascender. The ascender stem of the 'k' is like the 'h' and the diagonal thin stroke and the tail intersect just above the centre of the x height.

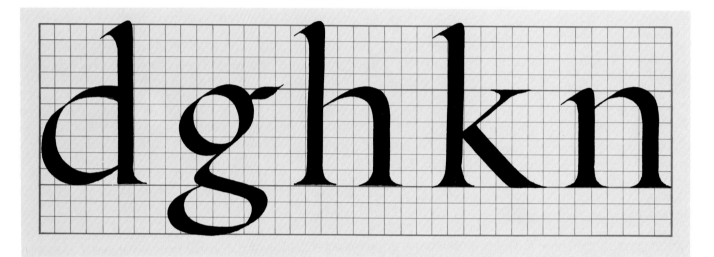

With the 'p', the join of the lower part of the bowl to the stem is somewhat flattened. A serif is attached to the bowl at the top left-hand corner. The 'q' is not a 'p' in reverse but is totally different in character, having no serif at the x line and with the upper stroke of the bowl being straightened to meet the stem.

The 'u' is not an inverted 'n'. The upper serifs protrude beyond the x line and a space is left where the curve makes its upward movement to meet the second stem. In the 'x', the point of intersection of the thin and thick strokes is above the x-height centre, making the lower counter larger than the upper. The diagonal thick stroke of the 'y' does not reach the base line but is intersected by the thin stroke, which follows through to the descender line where it ends in a flat, bracketed serif.

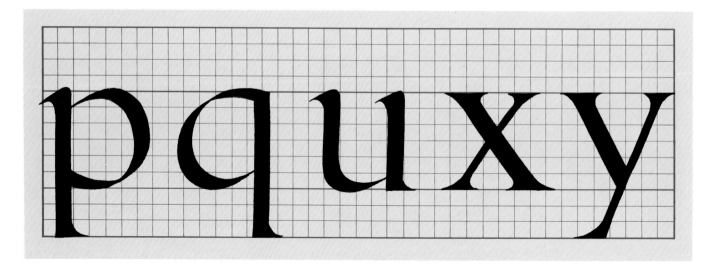

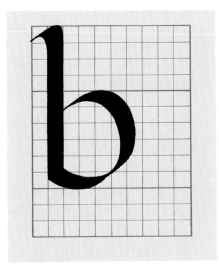

Group 3
The two letters in this group take up approximately six-and-a-half units in width. The 'b' is an ascending letter, the main stem swinging to the right before it meets the base line. The 'o' is contained within the x height with the exception of minor optical adjustments at the x and base lines.

Group 4
This group contains the 'a', 'c', 'e', 'f', 'v' and 'z' and, with the exception of 'f', they are all contained within the x height.

The 'a' starts from a pointed, curved arm which leads into the main stem. The bowl starts from the stem above the centre line of the x height and moves to the left before the downward curve. It rejoins the stem above the base line, leaving a triangular shape. The 'c' follows the left-hand stroke of the 'o', the upper arm being slightly straightened and ending in a sheared terminal which is extended to form a beak-like serif. The lower arm ends in a pointed terminal. The 'e' follows the 'c'; the upper arm, however, is not straightened but flows round. I end the stroke obliquely. The bowl is formed by a cross-stroke which is positioned above the x-height centre.

The 'f' is an ascending letter, starting its main stroke below the ascender line with the arm projecting to the right and ending in a sheared beak-like serif. The cross-bar is positioned just below the x line. The 'v' and 'z' both follow the same construction as their capital counterparts.

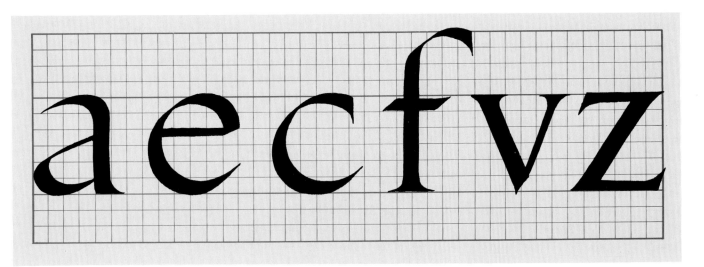

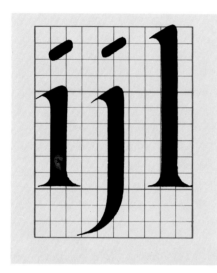

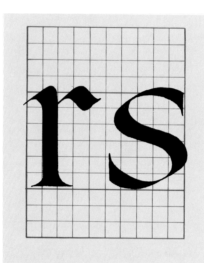

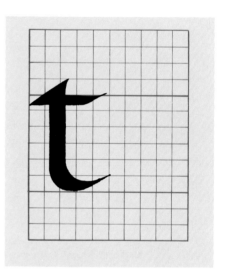

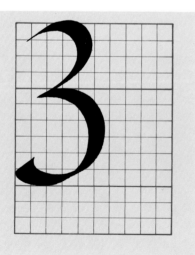

Group 5

This grouping contains three characters, about five units wide: the 'r', 's' and 't'. From the main stem of the 'r' there is a small shoulder stroke which should not be overdone — if it is too long it can interfere with the lettering of the character which follows. The 's' is constructed in the same manner as its capital.

The main stem of the 't' starts obliquely, a little way above the x line, moving to the right before reaching the base line and ending in a pointed terminal. Like the 'f', the cross-stroke is finished with a slight upwards movement.

Group 6

The 'i', 'j' and 'l' fall into this narrow-letter group. They are easily constructed, with the humble 'i' and 'l' setting the pattern for straight letters. The dot over the 'i' and 'j' can be round or flat and is usually positioned about midway between the x and ascender lines. The 'j' initially follows the 'i' but extends below the base line where it curves to the left, ending in a pointed terminal.

NUMERALS

The Romans used letters of the alphabet for their numeric reference. We are all familiar with the Roman-style numerals when applied to a clock face, but perhaps not so with M = 1,000, D = 500, C = 100 and L = 50. It takes little imagination to see that mathematical calculations could be made easier by changing the symbols. The Arabs did exactly that and based their system on 10 numeric signs, the 'Arabic numerals' we use today. They can be either of uniform height ('lining numerals') or of varying height ('old style' or 'hanging numerals'). In the latter style the 1, 2 and 0 appear within the x height, the '6' and '8' are ascending numerals and the 3, 4, 5, 7 and 9 are descending characters.

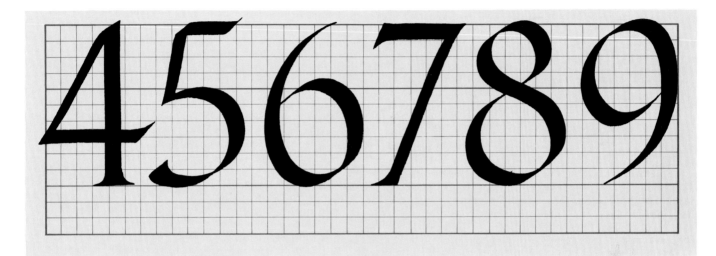

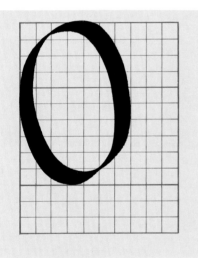

The main characteristics of the numerals need little explanation, but a few points should be noted. For example, if numerals are not constructed carefully they can appear to be falling over. This, I feel, is because they are mainly asymmetric in form, with the exception of the 0, 1 and 8, which are basically balanced.

If the curve of the 2 is allowed to project beyond the base cross-stroke, it will appear to be leaning to the right. If the tail of the 9 is not carried sufficiently far to the left, the figure will appear to lean to the left; if too far, it will look as if it is leaning to the right. The 9 is not an inverted 6. The join of the small curved stroke to the main curved stem alters in each case, making the inner counters slightly different in shape.

The upper counters of the 3 and 8 should be smaller than the lower; otherwise the characters will be top heavy. The cross-bar of the 4 is fairly low on the stem so that the inner counter does not appear too small. The diagonal stroke of the 7 cannot extend too far to the left: once it goes beyond the alignment of the upper stroke, it makes the letter look as if it were leaning backwards. If the cross-stroke of the 5 is too long, it too can appear to lean to the right. Finally, it should be noted that the numeral 0 is compressed and not a letter 'O'.

Within our written language there are of course many other symbols such as parentheses, exclamation marks and question marks, to name but a few. These will become natural enough to create once the student starts practising calligraphy.

The character '&' is known as the ampersand. This is possibly a corruption of the mixed English and Latin phrase 'and *per se* and'. It is an ancient monogram of the letters 'e' and 't', the Latin word *et* meaning 'and'. The *et* in this instance is not reflected in the character on the grid, which occupies nine units in width. The upper bowl is much smaller than the lower with the angle of the diagonal stroke cutting through to form a semicircular counter and the tail ending in a bracketed serif. The upward tail to the bowl ends with a bracketed serif above the centre line.

24

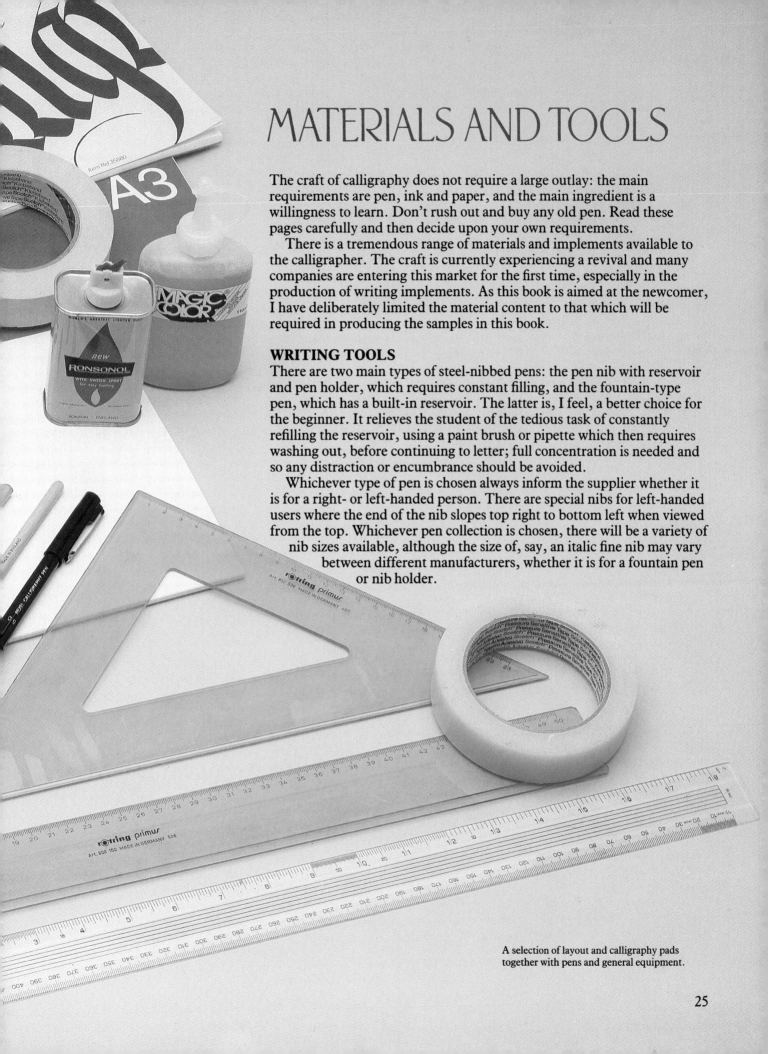

MATERIALS AND TOOLS

The craft of calligraphy does not require a large outlay: the main requirements are pen, ink and paper, and the main ingredient is a willingness to learn. Don't rush out and buy any old pen. Read these pages carefully and then decide upon your own requirements.

There is a tremendous range of materials and implements available to the calligrapher. The craft is currently experiencing a revival and many companies are entering this market for the first time, especially in the production of writing implements. As this book is aimed at the newcomer, I have deliberately limited the material content to that which will be required in producing the samples in this book.

WRITING TOOLS

There are two main types of steel-nibbed pens: the pen nib with reservoir and pen holder, which requires constant filling, and the fountain-type pen, which has a built-in reservoir. The latter is, I feel, a better choice for the beginner. It relieves the student of the tedious task of constantly refilling the reservoir, using a paint brush or pipette which then requires washing out, before continuing to letter; full concentration is needed and so any distraction or encumbrance should be avoided.

Whichever type of pen is chosen always inform the supplier whether it is for a right- or left-handed person. There are special nibs for left-handed users where the end of the nib slopes top right to bottom left when viewed from the top. Whichever pen collection is chosen, there will be a variety of nib sizes available, although the size of, say, an italic fine nib may vary between different manufacturers, whether it is for a fountain pen or nib holder.

A selection of layout and calligraphy pads together with pens and general equipment.

An Osmiroid B4 left-hand nib unit and an Osmiroid B4 right-hand nib unit.

Three kinds of fountain-type pens. Both the Osmiroid and Platignum have a variety of interchangeable nib units. The Rotring art pen is a complete unit, available in a number of metric sizes.

The ink holders, or reservoirs, are of either the squeeze or piston type and all three pens have an optional cartridge ink supply..

Fountain-type pens

There are various calligraphic pens on the market. Some are purchased as an integral unit (that is, a complete pen); others are bought as a set and include a barrel, reservoir and a set of interchangeable nib units. Avoid the cartridge refill as it limits the colour of ink that can be used. It is better to buy a pen which has a squeeze-fill reservoir so that colour can be changed quite easily.

Don't be afraid to ask the local art shop or stationers to show their entire range. The larger suppliers often have demonstration pens that can be tested before finally making a decision to purchase.

The choice of pens available is ever-increasing and I have used many different makes of pen. The one on which I have become reliant and have used since my college days is an Osmiroid. It suits my style and I feel comfortable using it. However, the choice is yours.

Pen holders and inks

Once the student has gained confidence and experience with a pen, a pen holder and range of nibs is the next addition to any calligrapher's equipment. The range available is vast, including round-hand, script, poster, scroll and special-effect nibs. These items are sold separately or can often be bought on a display card which contains pen holder, reservoir and set of nibs. If a student does decide to purchase this type of pen he will need to remove the film of lacquer with which the nibs are coated to avoid deterioration. This can be done either by passing the nib through a flame briefly or by gently scraping the surface.

A selection of nibs from the Rexel range.

Rexel pen nibs and holders with an ink reservoir and Speedball nibs (with integral reservoir) and holder.

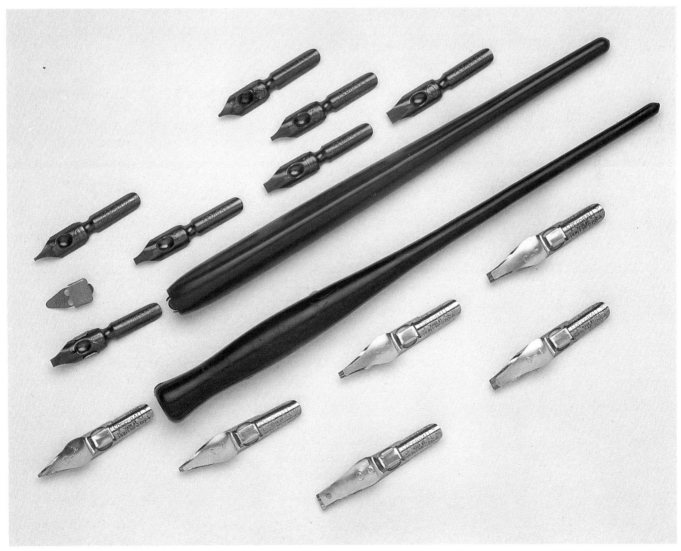

INKS

There are many inks available to the student, and choice is made difficult by this fact. The main property an ink should have is that it should flow easily and not clog the pen. Non-waterproof ink flows marginally better than waterproof inks and watercolours. The medium should not spread on the writing surface. Unwanted feathering can be attributed either to the paper or to the ink, and the student should experiment with both to confirm compatibility.

Density of colour is important in finished work, and there are inks available which are specifically stated as being calligraphic inks. These are suitable for use in fountain-type pens. There are also inks that are referred to as 'artist colour', some of which are waterproof; many need a cleaning fluid to clean or flush the pen through after use. (Check with the stockist that such a cleaning agent will have no harmful effects.) The range of colours is wide, and most of these types of ink are miscible, giving an even wider range.

Calligraphers often use watercolour paint for embellishment. This is satisfactory for a pen and holder but not for a fountain pen. Instead of watercolour, pens can be filled with artists' retouching dye, which is translucent and the colour is very pure and water soluble. Ink and watercolours vary in light fastness; so check the label for the product's degree of permanence.

Some bottles have a pipette incorporated in the cap. This is useful for charging the reservoirs in pen holders and saves loading with a brush.

PAPER

For the beginner, a draughtsman's or designer's layout pad is ideal for roughing out ideas and preliminary penwork. Pads come in various sizes, finishes and weights. Initially, choose a paper that is not too opaque and make sure, when the paper is placed over the sample alphabets in this book, that you can still see the letterforms through it.

There are typo pads specifically made for designers' layouts. This type of pad is ideal, because it is used for tracing letters in studios when laying out work. It has a slightly milky appearance and is not as transparent as tracing paper.

For finished work a good quality cartridge paper is ideal. Writing papers are produced in many shades and finishes, although they can be a little restrictive due to the sizes available. There are also many drawing papers which can be put to good use. It is as well to experiment with different types of paper, avoiding those with a heavy coating, as they will obstruct the passage of the nib and the flow of the ink. For outdoor work such as posters, special papers that weather well can be used, but do not forget to use a waterproof ink.

Ingres paper for finished work, available in pads or single sheets.

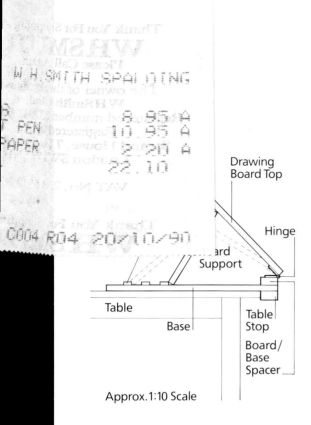

Drawing
Board Top

Hinge

ard
Support

Table

Base

Table
Stop

Board/
Base
Spacer

Approx.1:10 Scale

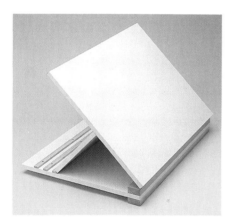

A home-made drawing board with three
adjustable angles.

A Trueline drawing board with parallel motion.

DRAWING BOARD

A drawing board on which to work will of course be required. This need
not be an expensive purchase. In calligraphy, work is carried out with the
drawing board at an angle. The student should be positioned in front of
the work so that he can see it clearly without stretching. The angle of the
board should ideally be about 45°. However, providing the calligrapher is
in a good viewing position, it may be as low as 30° – whatever suits the
individual. Never work on a flat surface as this necessitates bending over
the board and using the pen in an upright position, whereas on a sloping
board the pen is at a shallower angle, helping to regulate the ink flow.

A drawing board can be purchased, with or without adjustable angles,
from most art shops. Alternatively, laminate shelving board is available at
most timber merchants and is quite adequate. A suitable board size is 18
× 24 in (450 × 600 mm). Apply iron-on laminate edges to give a clean
finish. The board can be supported on one's lap and leant against a table
or desk, making an angle of about 45° with the desk top. A professional-
looking board that adjusts to three angles can be made quite readily. The
board illustrated is approximately one-tenth scale and therefore all
measurements will require multiplying by ten.

Cut two laminate boards to the dimensions above, one for the base and
the other for the top. In the same material cut a further piece for the board
support and some softwood for support battens, table stop and board-base
spacer. All these items measure the same width as the drawing board. In
addition six butt hinges and some chipboard screws will be required.

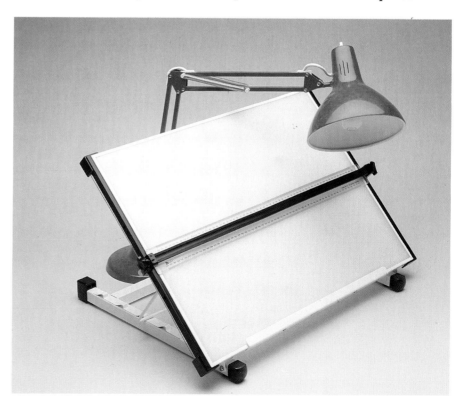

Screw a board spacer to one edge of the base together with a table stop on the opposite side to prevent the board from sliding when in use. Screw the support battens to the base in the positions shown to give three angles from 30° to 45° approximately.

Attach the board support to the drawing board top with three of the hinges, one in the centre and one a little distance in from each end. It is essential that the support is positioned correctly to achieve the desired angles. Fix the remaining three hinges to the drawing board, underside at the base, with the other side to the board-base spacer. Give all edges a clean finish with iron-on laminate.

RULER

Choose an 18 in (450 mm) ruler, preferably with both metric and imperial calibrations. Transparent rulers with grid lines running parallel to their edges can be useful for horizontal alignment in rough layouts, where multiple lines need ruling.

A ruler with a good bevelled edge is more accurate in transferring measurements and is useful when reversed for ruling ink lines as the bevelled edge prevents ink seeping under the ruler.

SET SQUARE

A 45° set square will be required. Some have millimetre calibrations on the right-angled edges, and these are useful when laying out rectangular shapes. The square should be at least 10 in (250 mm) on the two shorter edges. A smiliar 30°/60° set square will also be needed.

PENCILS

An H or 2H pencil is needed for preliminary guidelines, which need to be fine. The leads are not too soft; so the student won't be spending all his time keeping a keen point on the pencil.

An HB will be required for rough layout work as it is sufficiently soft to give a good image without unnecessary pressure. A soft carpenter's pencil is ideal for initial test layouts and can be sharpened to a chisel edge to emulate the size of calligraphic nib to be used.

Propelling, or clutch, pencils have become very popular in recent years, and HB, H and 2H leads are available. A $\frac{1}{50}$ in (0.5mm) lead size is preferable, as the smaller leads tend to snap easily.

ERASER

There are many erasers on the market. Choose a plastic one for paper and film.

CUTTING TOOL

A surgical scalpel is very useful and has an exceptionally keen edge. Replacement blades are sold in units of five per packet. Do be careful when changing the blade, which will be extremely sharp and should be treated with great respect. Always remove the blade by lifting it first from its retaining lug and then with the thumb, push the blade away from the body. Keep the fingers well away from contact with the cutting edge. When fitting a new blade, slide it on to the retaining lug, grip the blade on the blunt top edge and push it home. When the scalpel is not in use, a cork from your favourite bottle of wine will protect both you and the blade.

ADDITIONAL REQUIREMENTS

These include masking tape and a few large sheets of cartridge paper to cover the new board and to guard any work. Absorbent cloth, or kitchen roll, will also be necessary to wipe clean the fountain pen after filling and the nib when the ink shows signs of building up or clogging.

Some double-sided tape and a substantial weight of card will be required, as may additional lighting if the working area lacks sufficient daylight or good artificial light. Lighting is discussed in more detail in 'Setting up the drawing board'.

When the scalpel is not in use, use a cork to prevent accidents and avoid blunting the blade.

Ease the scalpel blade from its mounting using a thumbnail.

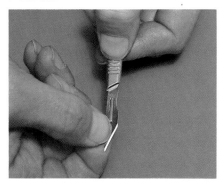

Place the new blade on the handle mounting.

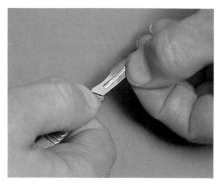

Pull the blade from the handle mounting by gripping the blunt edge.

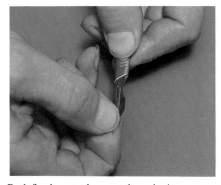

Push firmly on to the mounting gripping the blunt edge of the blade.

GENERAL HINTS ON MAINTENANCE

Emptying the ink from the pen.

For some, pens are not the easiest of implements to work with: they blot, dry up in the midst of a stroke or even refuse to write at all. However many of the complaints levelled at pens are due to poor maintenance. Just like any other tool, they need a certain amount of care and attention if they are to perform properly.

I would recommend that a fountain-type pen always be emptied of ink after use, unless it is to be re-used in a short space of time. Ink soon dries both on the nib and in the ink-feed section, rendering the implement useless. Time and effort can be saved by emptying the reservoir into the ink bottle and flushing the pen with lukewarm water which contains a drop of washing-up liquid. This simple measure is ideal for water-based inks and will keep the pen in good condition.

Occasionally it is necessary to strip down the whole nib unit and clean it with soapy water and an old tooth-brush or nail-brush. Most manufacturers would be horrified to think that such an act was necessary to clean their pens, but when changes of colour are required from, say, black to red, merely flushing the pen is insufficient to remove all the black ink, and the red or lighter colour will be tainted if the pen is not completely clean. If a pen has been left with ink inside for a period of time, without use, it will require stripping down in the same manner. A pipe cleaner is ideal for removing ink from inside the squeeze-type reservoirs, but make sure that its wire centre does not puncture the plastic.

Removing the nib and ink feeder from its housing.

Separating the nib from the ink feeder.

Washing out the housing and ink holder, or reservoir, in water.

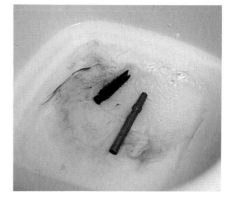

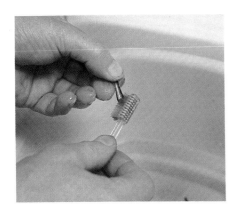

Using a toothbrush soaked in cleaning fluid to clean the parts.

Using a pipe cleaner soaked in fluid to remove all the ink from inside the ink holder or reservoir.

There are now many different waterproof inks available for use in fountain-type pens. The colour range available is so vast that most students cannot wait to try them out. The snag about waterproof inks is that, once the pen is left for a short time, a waterproof ink will dry up and be difficult to remove with a water-based solution.

There is a cleaner available which is primarily used by airbrush artists for removing the colour from the airbrush. I have found this solution to be ideal for a thorough strip-down operation. The fluid has no harmful effect on the pen and removes even the hardened ink, but it is always best to ask the supplier if it is safe to use on plastics.

If the ink stops in the middle of a stroke, remove the barrel and squeeze or turn the reservoir, depending on the type of pen, until the ink reaches the nib. Make sure you have a paper towel at hand to prevent a disaster.

A pen that is drying or missing during writing may have insufficient ink, or the split in the nib may have become widened by pressure. To solve this problem either fill the pen or reduce the split in the nib by squeezing both sides together. Also check that the nib and ink duct are free from particles picked up from the paper surface. Ink will not take to a greasy surface. To remove such marks a good proprietary lighter fuel may be used. Test a sample of the same paper to ensure that the petrol does not leave a stain.

Rulers and set squares (triangles) should be cleaned only with warm soapy water. Abrasive cleaners will damage the plastic and remove the calibrations.

Aligning the nib and ink feeder before re-assembling the pen.

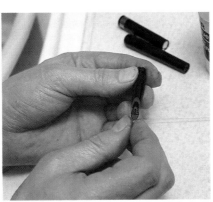

GETTING STARTED

The student should now have a basic understanding of letter construction and the necessary tools and materials to commence calligraphic lettering. The styles compiled in the following sections are basic calligraphic forms, but this certainly does not mean that they are easy. The student will require determination, patience and, in order to maintain concentration, peace and quiet.

I intend to make the learning of the subject as simple as possible. I have, in my lessons at calligraphic class, cut the learning time down by employing methods that are not altogether accepted in some teaching circles. Nevertheless, the students I have worked with have achieved an awareness of letterforms and have made rapid progress, becoming proficient with a pen very quickly; I therefore hope that the learning principles laid down in this book are adhered to. If I ask for a certain standard to be maintained — for example, accurate laying out of guidelines for lettering — the instructions should be followed carefully: the use of blunt pencils to mark these out would be unacceptable because it would produce inaccuracies.

I am, therefore, asking for the student to 'go by the book'. Wherever possible, time-saving devices have been incorporated to assist progress. So do not try to take short cuts. This invariably ends up with the student having to back-track. I have tried to indicate where the student could go wrong, in order to avoid unexpected disappointment and encourage perseverance. Students experiencing problems should check that they

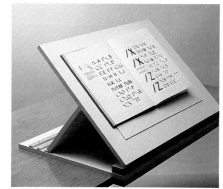

A card support with book in position for right-handed students.

A card support for left-handed students.

have followed the instructions correctly. I am convinced that most people can letter well, when properly guided.

SETTING UP THE DRAWING BOARD TO TRACE

The drawing board now has to be set up so that the book can be used as a tracing reference. Right-handed students should take a strip of heavy mounting card and position it with tape on to the writing surface. This is to rest this book on when the letterforms in the first sample are traced.

For left-handed students the card is positioned differently, because it is difficult for left-handed calligraphers to letter horizontally. The writing hand obscures the lettering produced and, even with a left-handed nib, to achieve the correct angle of writing can involve an uncomfortable pen hold. By tilting the paper the problem is lessened.

Therefore, left-handed students could try positioning the work with its right-hand side dropped down 15° from the horizontal, with the extra piece at right angles to prevent the book from sliding to the right. The student can then try lettering a few characters. If the position is uncomfortable the angle may need to be adjusted several times.

Once lettering exercise 1 has been tried, the student might find that by merely turning the paper through various degrees, he is still unable to achieve the desired angle of lettering. He should then resort to grinding down the nib to form an even steeper angle. This can be done on a fine-grade India stone or fine-grade production paper (the type used by car sprayers in the preparation of paintwork).

To save undue expense, experiment first with a nib used with a pen holder before attempting to convert a fountain-pen nib. This way, at least, if the result is not satisfactory, a relatively costly nib will not have been ruined. Make sure that when grinding down the edge, a burr is not left on one side, nor the edge left so sharp as to cut into the surface of the paper to be lettered. Finally, ensure that the edge of the nib is square, not rounded.

Applying padding to drawing board.

SETTING UP THE DRAWING BOARD FOR GENERAL WORK

Remove the pieces of card used to retain the book. Take two sheets of cartridge paper and cut them to a size which is 3 in (75 mm) less than the height and width of the surface area of the drawing board. If the board has been constructed from the illustration in this book, 15³⁄₁₆ × 21 in (385 × 535 mm) will be required. Place these sheets on the board surface with an equal border all around of about 1½ in (40 mm). Using masking tape, stick both sheets together to the board. It will be easier if this is done with the board flat. Attach one of the long edges of the sheets first, then pull the sheets taut and stick down the opposite side. Then tape the two exposed ends.

For the pad cut a further, slightly larger, sheet of cartridge which will give a border of 1 in (25 mm) on the drawing board and stick this with tape on all four edges so that no edge is left exposed and the sheet is taut.

This will now provide an ideal writing surface. The pen does not perform well against a hard, solid surface and the backing sheets give a little spring, which is suited to the action of the nib. Once exercise 1 and the first alphabet have been lettered, the student should have a good idea of the point on the board where he feels most comfortable when lettering. This position will differ with the individual and is known as the writing level.

To prevent grease from the hand being deposited on the writing sheet, make a guard sheet from a sheet of cartridge paper. It must be positioned with tape on to the pad at a level that allows the student to work on his writing line.

To retain the writing sheet as it is moved towards the top of the board at the end of each line of lettering, a strip of fabric tape or card may be used at the top of the board. This is an optional extra; I prefer the sheet to be mobile, but I do recognize the strip's value when writing on material that has a tendency to curl.

Always put aside a spare piece of the writing material being used to start the pen off and to practice strokes.

Applying cover to drawing board.

LIGHTING

Correct lighting is as important for the eyes as posture is for the limbs. Tired eyes and limbs are not conducive to clean, crisp calligraphy. Ideally the student should work in daylight. If he is right-handed, the light source should be from the left, and if left-handed, from the right. Light, correctly directed, should ensure that the calligrapher is not working in his own shadow cast by the writing hand. Lighting therefore plays a key role in the laying out of the working area. Strong direct light, such as sunlight, should be avoided, as excessive glare from the usual white surface being worked will make lettering difficult.

The student will also need artificial light from an anglepoise lamp or similar unit, either wall-mounted or standing. The direction of the source is the same as for daylight. The advantage of an anglepoise lamp is that of ease of direction or position; for intricate work, light can be directed to the point required by simple adjustment.

THE POSITION TO ADOPT WHEN LETTERING

It is important to be comfortable when seated, with the feet flat on the floor, the back straight and the drawing board positioned so that the arms can move freely.

The height of the seat or chair used is important, and consideration should be given to the height of the table or desk on which the drawing board sits. If the board is too low, the calligrapher will inevitably acquire backache through bending over it; if too high, the neck and arms will suffer through constant stretching. The ideal height will differ for each student and adjustments to seating and height of drawing board may be necessary. I even know of one student who uses a foot stool in order to achieve a comfortable working position.

HOLDING THE PEN

It is important to hold the pen correctly between the thumb and first and second fingers, with the third and little fingers bent inwards towards the palm and resting on the writing surface. If this position is totally unnatural or uncomfortable then it may be necessary to resort to the usual method you adopted when writing.

There should be no tenseness and the hold must be relaxed. When writing, minimal pressure is required to form characters and to move the pen. The letterform's thick and thin characteristics are arrived at naturally through both the angle of the nib to the writing line and the direction the pen is moving in. This will be expanded upon with the first alphabet sample.

PEN PRACTICE

It is the angle of the nib in relation to the direction of writing and stroke which gives the letterforms their characteristics. A style that is formed with the nib angle at 30° to the writing line will have a different visual appearance to that lettered at 45°. This is because it is the angle that determines the weight of each stroke and the stress of the round letters. Because the angle is maintained from letter to letter, with the exception of one or two strokes, a certain quality and rhythm is created throughout the letterforms.

Because the pen angle is 30°, a vertical stroke will only be as wide as the image the nib will make at that angle and not equivalent to the full nib width. In a round letterform, there is a point at which the whole of the nib width is used due to the pen travelling in a semicircle.

The maximum width of stroke – 'the stress' – will be exactly 90° to the thinnest stroke, which is fortunate for round letterforms because, if the nature of the tool used did not produce this automatically, round letterforms would appear thinner than vertical ones of the same weight. Indeed, when letterforms are freely constructed with a pencil and filled in with a brush, compensation has to be made to the curved thick strokes,

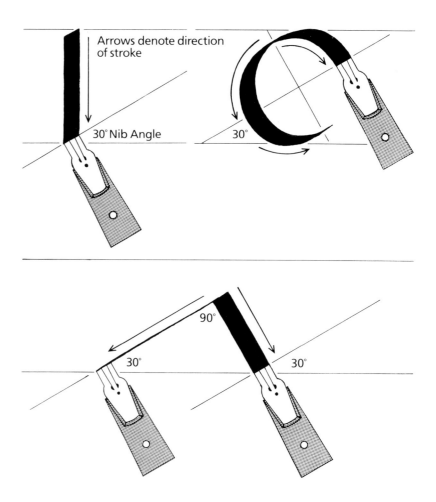

increasing them in weight to give an optical balance with straight strokes.

Weight of stroke is determined by the angle of the pen and the direction of travel. Diagonal strokes will vary in weight depending on the direction of the stroke. Strokes made from top left to bottom right are more consistent than those formed top right to bottom left. Horizontal strokes are of a uniform width. These variations are acceptable in pen lettering and give the forms a natural, unforced appearance. The alphabet is constructed from common vertical, horizontal, diagonal and curved strokes.

Letterforms within the alphabet have common likenesses and, although there are 26 characters, the strokes that are repeated within the capitals and lower case are frequent. This repetition makes the task easier: once the basic strokes used in letter construction are mastered, the forming of individual letters is relatively simple. The ability to produce the strokes with confidence comes from practising them on layout paper.

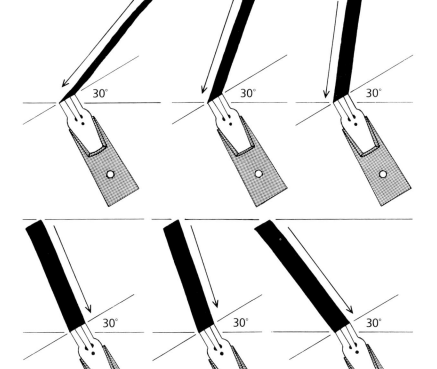

The width of stroke varies according to the direction in which the pen is moved while retaining a fixed nib angle.

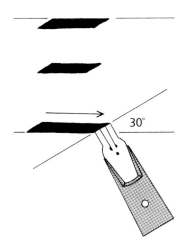

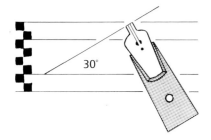

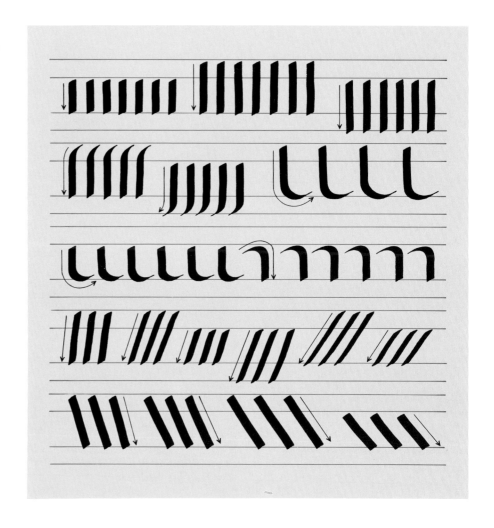

FORMING STROKES

Unlike handwriting, where the pen is lifted from the paper only occasionally between words or necessary breaks in form, calligraphic lettering dictates that the pen is lifted after each stroke. It is the combination of strokes which creates the letterforms.

The pen is nearly always used with a pulling action towards the letterer. Horizontal strokes are made from left to right. The nib should glide across the sheet with just enough pressure to keep it in contact with the writing surface.

It is at this point that problems often face the newcomer to calligraphy. It is essential that the pen angle is maintained while producing the stroke, whatever direction is taken. This usually takes all of the student's concentration and can result in the nib not being in contact with the paper throughout the movement. This skipping will cause an uneven weight in the stroke, and the result will be patchy.

Control over the pen for small letters is with the fingers for the up-and-down movements, with the wrist being employed only slightly for

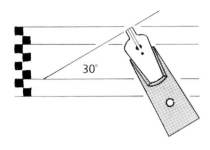

These simple strokes form the basis of letter construction.

rounded letters. When forming larger letters, say over ¾ in (20 mm), the movement is from the shoulder with the whole arm moving down the writing surface. The height of letter at which the transition from finger to arm movement is made is dependent upon the dexterity of the individual.

The exercise requires mainly finger and wrist action with, perhaps, some of the longer, diagonal strokes needing arm movement. The third and little finger rest on the paper and help to support the pen holder.

BASIC LETTER STROKES

Begin by tracing over the forms given in the exercise. To do this, a nib that is of the same size as that used here will be required. Take a nib and compare it with the nib and width of stroke marked at the side of the sample exercise. It will be beneficial if the size can be matched exactly, although a small variation will not matter at this stage. The main aim of the exercise is for the student to become familiar with the action of the pen and to develop a rhythm when forming the images.

PROPORTIONS IN PEN LETTERING

Before lettering the alphabet sample can commence, the basic proportions of calligraphic letterforms must be considered as must the method of arriving at a size of letter from a particular nib size.

The ratio of x height to capital height will vary from style to style. The first sample, Roman Sans Serif, has a different proportion from that of the Roman Hand. Proportions will differ between styles although the same size nib is used to produce each form. It is the proportion of the style which gives the main characteristic to the form; while the addition of serifs and flourishes are features which distinguish one style from another, they can almost certainly be regarded as adornment. The overall weight of an alphabet is based on width of nib to height of capitals and x height.

There are no hard-and-fast rules regarding proportion. Those used in this book are simplified to even units of nib width to make the student's task easier. However, once the styles are familiar, it may be of interest to experiment with slightly different proportions. For instance, the Roman Sans Serif sample could be lettered with an x height of five nib widths while still retaining two nib widths for ascenders and descenders, giving a lighter rendering of the letterforms overall. The student could then try 5½ nib widths with 2½ for ascenders and descenders. There is a limit in both increasing and decreasing the x height at which the style will become illegible and difficult to produce. Suffice to say that the porportions I have chosen are suitable for practical application, giving good legibility.

In calligraphy the proportion of a given style is based on the number of nib widths used for the capital height, the x height, and the ascender and descender areas.

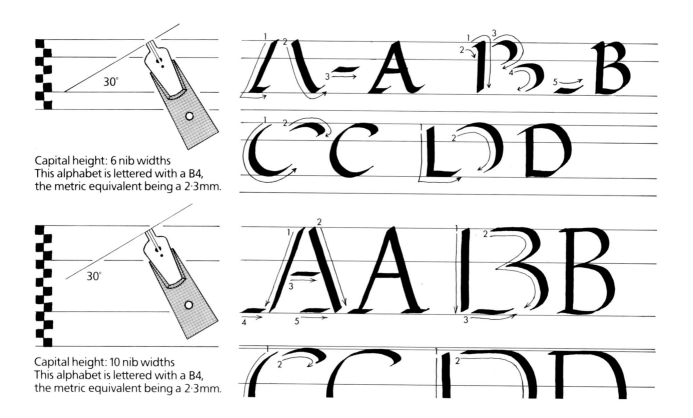

Capital height: 6 nib widths
This alphabet is lettered with a B4, the metric equivalent being a 2·3mm.

Capital height: 10 nib widths
This alphabet is lettered with a B4, the metric equivalent being a 2·3mm.

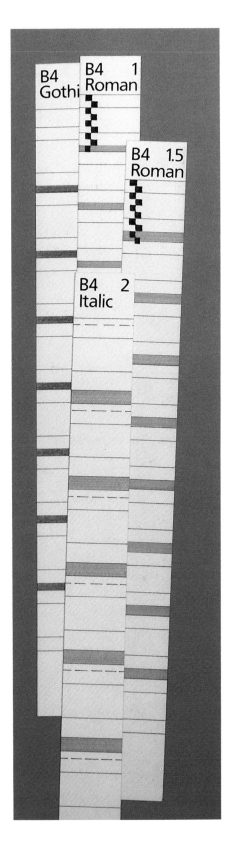

LAYING OUT GUIDE LINES

To begin with, look at the alphabet sample you wish to produce. All the samples in this book have a chequer-board pen width pattern which appears before the alphabet and indicates the proportions required to produce the alphabet, together with the adopted lettering angle at which the style should be executed.

The method for laying out the sheet for the first sample, Roman Sans Serif, is as follows. (This style has a capital height of six nib widths, x height of four nib widths, giving an ascender area of two nib widths and corresponding descender area of two nib widths.) Take a sheet of layout paper and draw a line parallel to the top of the sheet about 1½ in (40 mm) from the edge with a sharp 2H pencil. Take a pen that has an equivalent nib width to that used in the sample alphabet. I have used a B4 for most of the exercises in this book but a 2.3 mm nib is almost identical. From this base line step up six nib widths on the left of the sheet. They should be in a chequered pattern. The nib must be vertical to the writing line so that its full width is used when marking off. Now mark off three nib widths below the line, two for the descenders and the third for interlinear space.

Take a strip of cartridge paper about 1 in (25 mm) by 9 in (230 mm) and place it alongside the chequered pattern. Transfer the measurements, the capital line, x height line, base line, descender line and interlinear line; the units should be two, four, two and one respectively. Move the strip of card upwards so that the last line of interlinear area is at the capital line and repeat the process of transferring the measurements.

The card will hold 10 lines of lettering in all. It is a good idea to draw the lines across the strip so that each side of the marker can be used. To differentiate between lines of writing and interlinear space, mark an 'x' between the x height lines and colour or shade the interlinear areas.

The strip should also contain useful information such as the size of nib, the style for which it is to be used and the interlinear measurement. Cover the marker with clear adhesive tape, the type that does not discolour with age. I always tape the underside of the marker to keep it clean. A marker gauge now exists, which can be kept and used over and over again for transferring measurements for this nib size and alphabet. If a marker is made for each alphabet, it will reduce the time entailed in preliminary work.

Go back to the layout sheet and align the first base line with that of the marker, transfer the marker measurements to the sheet on the left-hand side and then move to the right-hand side of the sheet and repeat the process. Rule lines across the sheet to join up the measurements.

The beauty of the nib-width system for determining the height of lettering is quite simply that, irrespective of the nib size used, the proportions of the letterforms remain the same, provided that the nib widths are stepped off with the nib intended to do the lettering. Obviously a nib of half the width of that used to letter the first sample style would produce a lightweight rendering of that style.

A selection of marker gauges used when assessing depth of copy.

ROMAN SANS SERIF ALPHABET

Roman in this instance refers to a vertical style as opposed to an inclined style, which is called italic. It has no affinity with true Roman lettering which has serifs at the stem terminals. Sans Serif means without serifs, 'sans' translating from French and Latin as 'without'.

There are many type styles used in printing which are sans serif and they have become very popular in recent times. This style of lettering was popular in Victorian times and was often referred to as Grotesque lettering.

In calligraphy, the style is frowned upon, but I feel this is snobbery on the part of the scribes. It would appear that, unless letterforms are adorned with flourishes and serifs, they have little value in some

The Sans Serif style is ideal for conveying descriptive information in a clear manner. Here, the crispness of the alphabet has been combined with a delicate and technical approach to the illustration.

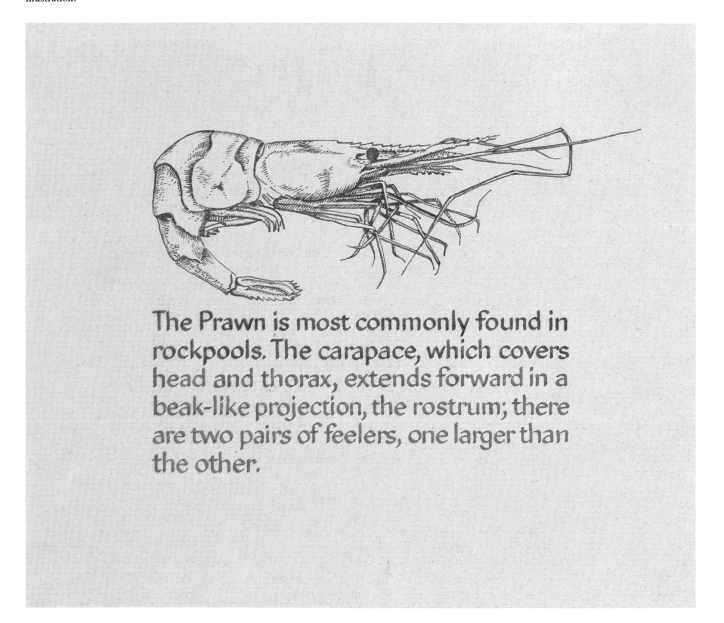

The Prawn is most commonly found in rockpools. The carapace, which covers head and thorax, extends forward in a beak-like projection, the rostrum; there are two pairs of feelers, one larger than the other.

calligraphers' portfolios, who are often more interested in fanciful letterforms than practical styles.

I have chosen this style for the introduction to lettering mainly because it is clean and crisp and requires the minimum of directional changes to form the letters. This does not imply that the style is simple to produce – far from it. The very nature of the alphabet is one of precision, requiring accuracy in construction and giving no cover for mistakes. By this I mean that there are no additional embellishments to distract the eye, so that the letters must be well formed if they are to be pleasing. Once the student has become proficient in producing this style, it will not be difficult to attain the additional movements necessary to create the other sample alphabets in this book.

Roman Sans Serif is a particularly useful style for handbills, posters, notices and the like, where communication is of the essence. It is an extremely legible style, giving high character recognition, and is easily adapted to condensing or expanding the forms, more of which will be explained later under 'Condensing or expanding a style'.

Choose a nib that is the same size as that used to letter the sheet – a B4 or $^3/_{16}$ in (2.3 mm). If unsure, take the nib and measure it against the pen drawing at the top of the column, as this is drawn to actual size. If the student does not possess a nib that is actual size, he will have to take the nearest to it and step off the nib widths as indicated under 'Proportions in pen lettering'. Then the guidelines should be drawn and the style copied. The pen angle is approximately 30° to the writing line. Set up the drawing for general calligraphic work and not for tracing.

If using a B4, take the book and lay it on the drawing board as for tracing. Take the layout sheet with pre-drawn guidelines and start by tracing the letterforms, not forgetting to use a guard sheet to keep the work free from grease and dirt. The sample alphabet shows the breakdown of strokes for the forming of each letter. The arrows denote direction of stroke and the numerals the order in which the strokes are produced. The majority of strokes are made with finger and wrist movement only. However, some of the longer diagonal strokes may require some arm movement, depending upon the dexterity of the individual. For the diagonal strokes of the 'Z', both capital and lower case, and also of the numeral '7', the angle of the pen has been changed to almost parallel to the writing line.

The nib must be kept in contact with the writing surface during the forming of any stroke, but it is lifted from the surface upon completion. Skipping is the result of the pen not being in contact with the paper. This can be recognized by an unevenness in straight strokes, where a thickening and thinning in stems appears, and by broken curves in round forms. Always draw the pen; never push the nib.

Once it is felt that the letterforms being produced resemble those in the sample, continue to produce the forms without tracing them. The drawing board must then be set up for general work and not tracing.

Keep the practice sheets even if it is felt that they are not up to standard. They will be a useful guide to check on progress and without doubt will give encouragement in the times when the student is questioning his own ability.

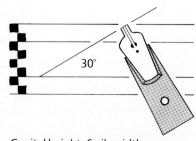

30°

Capital height: 6 nib widths
This alphabet is lettered with a B4,
the metric equivalent being a 2·3mm.

Nib Angle approximately 30°

Arrows denote direction of stroke.
Numerals indicate order of character
construction.

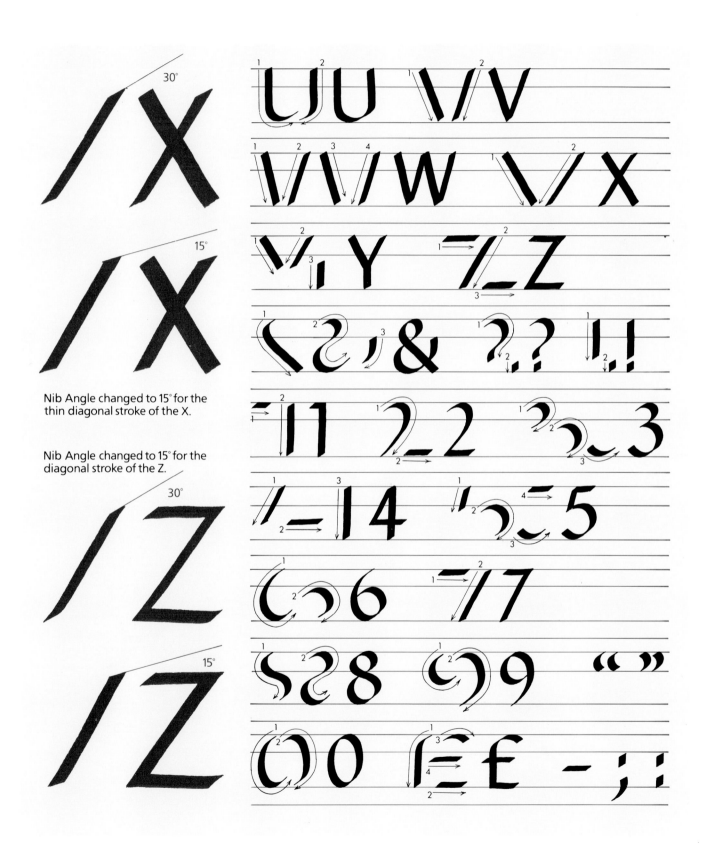

Nib Angle changed to 15° for the thin diagonal stroke of the X.

Nib Angle changed to 15° for the diagonal stroke of the Z.

Ascenders: 2 nib widths

'x' height: 4 nib widths

Descenders: 2 nib widths

LETTER SPACING

inn
INN

Straight letters - wide spaced

boo
BOO

Round letters - close spaced

reef
REEF

Open letters - fairly close spaced

avail
AVAIL

Oblique letters - close but variable

Once the student has lettered his first alphabet, it is necessary to consider spacing the letters in order to produce words. This would be an easy task if all the character shapes were either straight-sided or round, as then the same amount of space could be left between them. Unfortunately, the alphabet consists of many different shaped characters; measuring the same amount of space between characters does not produce an aesthetically pleasing word. Instead reliance must be placed on optical spacing and fine adjustments.

Letter spacing is one of the most difficult aspects of lettering. Calligraphy, signwriting, using pre-cut letters or lettering proper (that is, with a brush on paper or board), all these forms of communication require good letter spacing if they are to achieve their aim of informing in a legible and attractive manner.

The characters of the alphabet can be divided into four main groups: straight-sided, rounded, open and oblique. Some fall into more than one group; for instance, the capital and lower case 'C' are both rounded and open. As a guideline, think of round letters as being close-spaced and straight-sided letters as being the widest spaced. Consider these two groups. A vertical letter in its simplest form is the 'I' and a round letter the 'O'. If the combinations of IOOI and OIIO are looked at, the difference in spacing, can be seen. The first line lettered is spaced mathematically, the second optically. The difference is that optical spacing takes into account the nature of the 'O', with its round shape giving a greater amount of white area than a straight-sided letter. It is this counter-space which must be considered. The golden rule is not only to appreciate the shape of the letters but also the white areas that they create around them. These are just as important as the forms themselves, and the student cannot commit himself to a letterform without being concerned with the areas they create.

The aim of the letterer is to produce even areas of white space between the letterforms. This will take time to learn, and experience only comes through a rational approach to spacing. A letterform's space requirement must be evaluated before committing pen to paper in order to achieve harmony.

IOOI OIIO

IOOI OIIO

DETERMINING WHAT SPACE TO USE

Once the student has lettered his first two characters, he has set the criteria which will determine the spacing of all the letters that follow. If the first two characters are straight-sided, they should be lettered with sufficient space between them to accommodate the close spacing necessary for round letters which may follow. Without making this judgement prior to lettering, the rounded forms will be tightly spaced and may even touch each other if the first letters are very close. The reverse

INDOORS
INDOORS

can be said for two rounded characters at the beginning of a word. If they are spaced too far apart, the end result will be an over-spaced word because the straight letters will require extra space to appear optically balanced with their rounded partners.

DOODLING
DOODLING

Open and oblique letterforms vary in the amount of space they require in accordance with the word construction. However, as a rule, open letters are fairly closely spaced because the open counter has to be taken into consideration.

Owing to the letter combinations, the word TALE for example is difficult to space. There are numerous other combinations for which it is almost impossible to achieve total harmony in the spacing and where it is

WYVERN
WYVERN

Optically spaced: the shaded areas should appear equal.

necessary to resort to other methods, such as the forming of ligatures or the reduction of the length of stroke.

In the word TALE the cross-bar at the right of the 'T' overlaps the thin diagonal stroke of the 'A'. This is done to reduce the natural space made by both letters and will now set the optical standard for the remaining letters. In order to space the 'L', the area between the 'T' and 'A' must be evaluated and the same amount of space be left between the thick oblique stroke which forms the right of the 'A' and the vertical straight stroke of the 'L'. In order to space the 'E', cover up the 'T' with a piece of paper. This will allow you to concentrate on the positioning of the 'E' without being distracted by the 'T'. Letter the 'E' so that the space left between the 'L' and 'E' is equivalent in area to that between the 'A' and 'L'. If a longer word required spacing, it would be necessary to cover up the previous letter in each case, so that only two letters are visible at any given time, while deciding on the position of the third. This spacing system is known as the three-letter spacing method.

Draw the guidelines with a sharp pencil, 4H or 2H, on a layout sheet, using the proportions for Roman Sans Serif. Letter the following words without tracing: indoors, wyvern, crafty, thirty, effigy. Now compare them with the words in the right-hand column, which are lettered correctly. In the left-hand column the words have been lettered without minor adjustments so that the problems that the letter combinations create can be clearly seen. I have made the alterations necessary to achieve an evenly spaced word. These include reducing the arm of the 'r', undercutting diagonal strokes and substituting ligatures where required.

All preliminary layouts should be scrutinized and any adjustments to letterspacing should be clearly marked as a reminder when producing the finished work.

indoors
shorten arm of 'r'
reduce #

indoors

wyvern
shorten arm of 'r'
reduce # *reduce #*
under-cut oblique strokes.

wyvern

crafty
shorten arm of 'r' *form ft ligature*
reduce #

crafty

Thirty
shorten cross bar *form rt ligature*
reduce # *–# ( )up*

Thirty

effigy
form ffi ligature
reduce #

effigy

= Space
+# = More Space
–# = Less Space
( )up = Close up

52

WORD SPACING

The extension from a single word to a line of text requires word spacing, that is, the amount of space left between one word and another. Word spacing is strongly linked with letter spacing in that if too much space is left between words the rhythm of the line is broken, leading to poor readability. The amount of space used must be consistent if continuity is to be achieved. Therefore, it is necessary to have a unit of space which is regular throughout the line and a simple system to determine the amount of white to be left.

Again, there is no mathematical answer for achieving even units of space, as the letterforms differ in shape and optically vary in counter areas. Word spacing must therefore also be based on visual judgement by using a capital 'I' for space between words in capitals and a lower case 'i' for lower case words. These 'i's are letter spaced between the words to give the same optical value. In effect, a complete spacing system has now been outlined.

The words in a line of text should be treated as a complete word. In the example, a capital 'I' has been inserted between the words and high-lighted in red to illustrate the system. When a line of text is word-spaced, the 'I' should be lettered using a carpenter's pencil which has been sharpened to a chisel edge the width of the pen nib, simulating the pen stroke width. After a line is completed, erase the pencil to give the finished result. Once the student has become familiar with word spacing, he need no longer use the pencil.

Draw up guidelines on a layout sheet using the proportions for Roman Sans Serif. Letter the example using the above method and compare the results with the sample lettered here.

THEISPACINGITOIUSE

inItheIspacingIofIwords.

INTERLINEAR SPACING

When lettering more than one line of text it sometimes becomes necessary to add extra space between lines. This is known as interlinear space. The main reason for this additional space is to prevent the descenders of one line from clashing with the ascenders of the line below. Even half a nib width of space inserted between the lines can eliminate the problem.

Both legibility and readability are determined by sensitive spacing.

Both legibility and readability are determined by sensitive spacing.

The style of lettering used will affect the amount of space required. If the style has a large x height with small ascenders and descenders, it will need more interlinear space than a style that has a small x height with long ascenders and descenders. This is because the latter creates more open space between lines of text owing to its larger ascenders and descenders,

Continuous text requires discerning interlinear space.

Continuous text requires discerning interlinear space.

and thus requires minimal interlinear space – if any – provided, of course, that characters do not clash. In some instances, it may be possible to reduce the length of ascenders and descenders to avoid clashing, but this should be treated with caution where letterforms with short ascenders and descenders are concerned.

As a guide to the amount of interlinear space required, the space between x heights should never be less than the x height of the style being lettered. This rule obviously refers to large x height, small ascender and descender styles.

The Roman Sans Serif style falls into this category, having a four-nib-width x height and two-nib-width ascender and descender proportion. If the proportions were, instead, five-nib-width x height and two-nib-width ascender and descender, it would be necessary to insert interlinear space to give the lines optical room to communicate their message efficiently.

The readability of a text is dependent upon letter spacing, word spacing, line length and interlinear spacing. The eye travels along a text from left to right, scanning a line before moving down to read the following line. If interlinear space is insufficient, the eye has difficulty in moving down a line and it is easy to end up re-reading the line just finished. Nevertheless it is not always the space between the lines which produces this effect. Often the line length is too great, and the eye has to travel too far back to pick up the next line, resulting in the line being missed or the same line being read twice.

Letter spacing and word spacing have been covered from the practical viewpoint, but the reasons for specific space being used have not yet been discussed. The eye is conditioned to recognize letter patterns; that is, individual characters are not 'read' in a word, but rather the pattern that they create. The wide spacing of letters and words hinders the reading rhythm. The effect of over-spaced words is to make it difficult to follow the line and often the reader jumps to the line below. This normally happens when the word space is greater than that of the interlinear space. Always consider both when producing continuous text, making the reader's task an interesting path to follow, without these stumbling blocks that can quite easily be avoided.

As the amount of characters to the line is so important, it will be discussed again later. However, for the time being, if the student notes that between eight and twelve words per line is an acceptable length for readability, he will not go far wrong.

This piece of text is, perhaps, a little ambitious for the beginner. It illustrates clearly how words can be manipulated to create a graphic image. The illustration adds to the design and holds the text together.

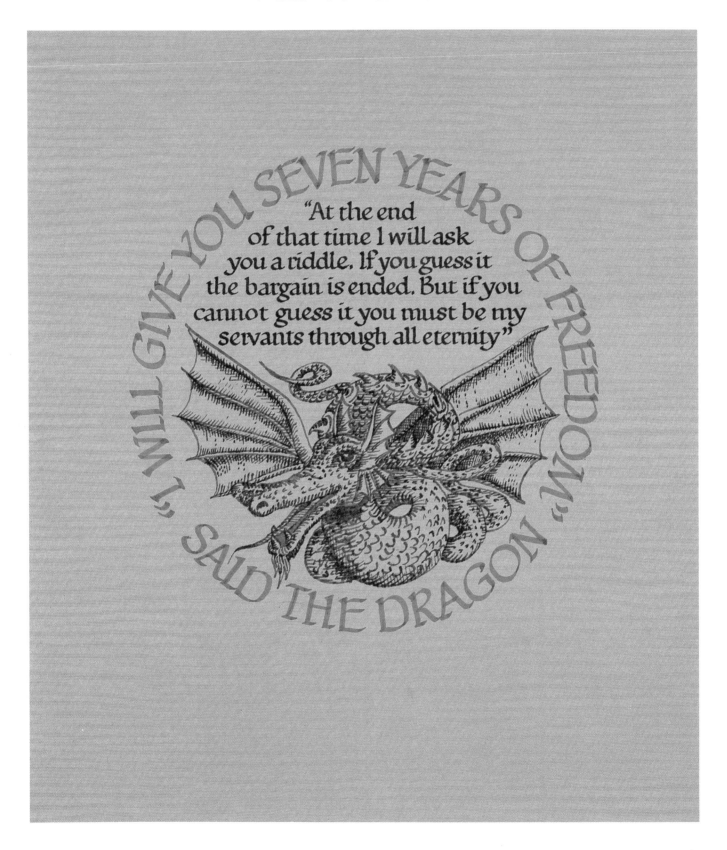

"AT the end
of that time I will ask
you a riddle. If you guess it
the bargain is ended. But if you
cannot guess it you must be my
servants through all eternity"

"I WILL GIVE YOU SEVEN YEARS OF FREEDOM," SAID THE DRAGON "I"

This style is based on Edward Johnston's Foundational Hand, which was modified from a 10th-century manuscript. In construction it is similar to Roman Sans Serif, but with the addition of serifs to give the style its character. These serifs are formed either by a change of direction, as in the serif at the foot of the thin diagonal stroke of the 'A', or by a second curved stroke into the main stem, such as that at the cap line of the 'B'. There are also tapered terminals, which are formed by a curving of the stroke ending at the pen angle, giving a point. This can be seen in the main stem of the 'A'.

The alphabet is lettered at an angle of 30° throughout with the exception of the capitals 'N', 'X' and 'Z'. The angle for both vertical strokes of the 'N' has been changed to 45° to give a slightly thinner stroke. The thin diagonal stroke of the 'X' has been lettered at 15° from the horizontal in order to give the stroke some body and keep it more in line with the thin diagonal strokes of the 'V' and 'W'. The 'Z' is the only letter that, when lettered with a 30° angle, has a main diagonal stem which is less in weight than the horizontal strokes. I feel that this anomaly should be overcome and have therefore adjusted the angle to 15° from the horizontal to give the stroke some stature. The lower case 'z' also requires this change.

As a guide, if the main strokes of any letter are regarded as being the trunk of a tree, then all other strokes emanating from the stem should be of a weight that the main stem can support. This, I hope, explains my concern with the letter 'Z'. All these above adjustments have been made to give the letters concerned a better relationship with other characters – to achieve harmony and continuity.

However carefully the letterforms are drawn, there will undoubtedly be a slight deviation from the 30° angle. Provided that it is only minor, it will not measurably affect the end result.

The guidelines should be drawn as indicated at the top of the first page of the alphabet. The numerals fall within the x height area but the student can, if he wishes, increase the size to that of the capitals. However, I prefer them slightly smaller. Most of the characters are lettered with finger movement only, although the longer strokes may need some arm movement coming from the shoulder.

Once the alphabet in its present form has been mastered, the student may wish to letter the style in the following proportions.

	ascenders	x height	descenders
nib widths	2	4¼	2
nib widths	2½	5	2½

This exercise is well worth the effort as it will show how a letterform changes in character when minor proportional adjustments are made. The alphabet style should, nevertheless, retain its general appearance and flavour once the nib values are changed. The overall effect of the proportional changes would be to make a page of text appear lighter.

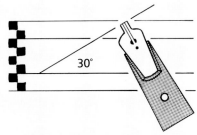

Capital height: 6 nib widths
This alphabet is lettered with a B4,
the metric equivalent being a 2·3mm.

Nib Angle approximately 30°

Arrows denote direction of stroke.
Numerals indicate order of character
construction.

Nib Angle changed to 45° for the
vertical strokes of the N.

Nib Angle changed to 15° for the diagonal stroke of the Z.

Nib Angle changed to 15° for the thin diagonal stroke of the X.

60

Ascenders: 2 nib widths

'x' height: 4 nib widths

Descenders: 2 nib widths

za a hb c c

cld ee f f

g g hh ii

j j kk ll

mm nn o

p p q r r

s s t uu

v v w w

z x y y z z

30°

15°

LAYOUT AND DESIGN

The layout and design of a text is governed by many factors. Legibility is a high priority and essential if the work is to communicate effectively. This is in turn dependent upon the size of letterform and length of written line, which in themselves are directly related to each other and to the size of the finished work.

A centred layout.

A ranged-left layout.

'What are moon-letters?'
asked the Hobbit full
of excitement. He loved
maps, as I have told
you before; and he also
liked runes and letters,
and cunning hand-
writing, though when
he wrote himself it was
a bit thin and spidery.

From "The Hobbit" by J.R.R.Tolkien

'What are moon-letters?'
asked the Hobbit full
of excitement. He loved
maps, as I have told
you before; and he also
liked runes and letters,
and cunning hand-
writing, though when
he wrote himself it was
a bit thin and spidery.

From "The Hobbit" by J.R.R.Tolkien

Aesthetic and creative qualities must also be considered, together with the stamp of the calligrapher's personality. The writing surface and texture used should be taken into account; colour and illustrative matter can also have a significant effect. All or some of these elements will require consideration before a layout can be produced.

If overall design appears to be a daunting task, with so many variables to equate before putting pen to paper, I can give some encouragement: only one or two aspects are evaluated at any given time. The principles behind layout and design can best be described as a process of elimination, a system of question and answer, which eventually leads the layout artist, calligrapher or designer to a solution to the given problem.

In the first instance the problem must be defined. This can easily be achieved by asking one question. What is the function of the piece of work? The answer is the starting point for the process of layout and design. The variables that pertain to the work can then be investigated.

There are five main types of layout generally used, although there are always artistic variations and combinations. These can be grouped as: ranged left; centred; ranged right; justified; and asymmetrical.

Ranged-left layout

Here the text is lettered flush to a left-hand margin, leaving the right-hand side ragged, that is to say the line lengths fluctuate. This layout is now used for all manner of work from quotations and poems to posters and invitations, and even manuscripts. The lettering in this type of layout is unforced, with word spacing of an even nature, and, because the wording for each line starts at the same position, it is relatively easy to produce. We are all conditioned from an early age to align text to a left-hand margin.

Centred layout

This is probably regarded as the classical way in which to display text, from invitations to fairly lengthy works. This symmetrical method of layout is both dignified and enduring and almost gives the work a stamp of approval. I would say that if the student is in doubt about the way in which a layout should appear, then centre it. Few people will comment adversely on a well-balanced piece of work: it projects harmony and not discord. To produce a centred layout requires both accuracy and patience because the individual lines of a text must be lettered twice – once on a rough layout to establish a line length and discover where breaks in the copy occur, and then again for the final work. The necessary procedures will be discussed in more detail later on in this section.

Ranged-right layout

This layout is not chosen very often but can be effective on posters. It is usually used in conjunction with other graphic elements, where the text ranges with a drawing, photograph or similar device. Because the text is aligned vertically on the right-hand side, it is difficult to produce. The ending of each line must be accurate if the text is to align. As with centred layouts, the lettering must be written initially on a rough layout.

A ranged-right layout.

'What are moon-letters?' asked the Hobbit full of excitement. He loved maps, as I have told you before; and he also liked runes and letters, and cunning hand-writing, though when he wrote himself it was a bit thin and spidery.

From "The Hobbit" by J.R.R.Tolkien

'What are moon-letters?'
asked the Hobbit full of
excitement, He loved
maps, as I have told you
before; and he also liked
runes and letters, and
cunning handwriting,
though when he wrote
himself it was a bit thin
and spidery.

From "The Hobbit" by J.R.R. Tolkien

Justified layout

A justified layout, or squared-up text, has to be the most arduous layout of all to produce. It requires accuracy at both the left- and right-hand margins, although justified text is more easily managed in a wide measure (the width of a column or line length) than in a narrow one. The letterforms and word spacing in each line have to be altered slightly to fit the measure. Because the line length is so short in a narrow column, each line has to be condensed or expanded in order to achieve a squared-up alignment on the left- and right-hand sides, sometimes resulting in drastic action. In order to produce the layouts, each line should be lettered several times before the correct width of character and spacing is arrived at. This is not a layout for the beginner, but is essential for some manuscript work if a book-like quality is needed. The main consideration when producing justified work is that of line length. Aim for at least seven to eight words on each line, which will make the task easier.

A justified layout.

'What are moon-letters?'asked the Hobbit
full of excitement, He loved maps, as I
have told you before; and he also liked
runes and letters, and cunning handwriting, though when he wrote himself
it was a bit thin and spidery.

From "The Hobbit"   By J.R.R. Tolkien

'What are moon-letters?'
asked the Hobbit
full of excitement.
He loved maps,
as I have told you before;
and he also liked
runes and letters,
and cunning handwriting,
though when
he wrote himself
it was a bit thin
and spidery.
From "The Hobbit" by J. R. R. Tolkien

An asymmetrical layout.

Asymmetrical layout

This is used quite often in the name of artistic licence. I have seen some stunning examples of non-aligning text, but I feel that its use is limited and it should only be employed with caution. It is difficult to give rules on how to produce such a layout as so much is dependent on an individual's feel for balance and shape.

DECIDING ON A TEXT AREA

There are traditional margin proportions which have been used for many years in the laying out of single sheets and double-page spreads. The unit values of head, foredge, foot and inner (or spine) margins were based on proportions of the quarto and octavo folds of given sheet sizes. In the UK, a full-size sheet of any size is called a Broadside; a Broadside folded in half is called a Folio; a Folio folded in half, making four sheets, is called Quarto and a Quarto folded in half, making eight leaves, is called an Octavo. Sheets of approximately the same sizes are available internationally. Today, paper sizes have been rationalized, which eliminates the problem of recalling dimensions when given a name of a sheet size and then having to work out the set margins.

When deciding on the size of sheet to use for a specific project, and the layout and margins to be used, the amount of text and the nature of the work must be taken into account. This section is devoted to continuous text and the margin proportions and width of measure which relate to this particular aspect of layout. The proportions given here will be adequate for most works and are given as a point from which to start laying out text. They can be changed to suit a particular requirement, but remember, when changing the unit values, to allow more space at the foot so that the column of text does not look as if it is slipping off the sheet area. Students always have some doubt when they first venture into the realms of layout and design but, with practice, they soon become proficient at decision-making.

Take a sheet 8¼ in (210 mm) by 5⅞ in (149 mm), which is known in the UK as A5, taken from the paper size A system (note pad size in the US). A5 is used for leaflets and brochures. The A system is unique, as the sheet proportion remains in the same ratio even when folded in half or doubled up in size.

To decide on a text area, the width of the A5 sheet, 5⅞ in (149 mm), must be divided by 10 to obtain a unit width, that is 14.9 mm. Round this up to the nearest whole millimetre to 15 mm. (Clearly, in this example it is easier to use the metric measure.) This will be the basic unit and it will be used to create the margins and text area of the sheet. One unit should be left at the head of the sheet, one unit for both the foredge and the spine and 1½ units at the foot. This leaves a text measure of 119 mm in width and 172 mm in depth. As a proportional system of arriving at a measure and depth of text, this principle of dividing by 10 and using the unit for margins works well on most sizes of sheet.

The size of text can be dependent on the amount of copy to be contained within the format, but emphasis here will be put on continuous

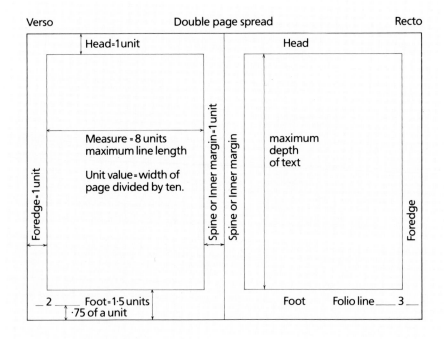

text, as in a manuscript or booklet of several pages. The golden rule in continuous text lettering is that the optimum in readability is a line-length of ten words. In the English language this is equivalent to 60 characters, as the average word is six characters long, including word spaces. Therefore the line length can be between eight and twelve words, or 48 and 72 characters. Given this information a nib size can be chosen to give approximately 60 characters to the line in the letter style decided upon. A typewritten manuscript can be easily fitted by counting the characters in one line, multiplying this by the number of lines and dividing the result by the number of characters contained within one line of the layout.

I have used Roman Serif for the example and tested various nib sizes – B2, Italic Broad, Italic Medium and Italic Fine – finally settling on Italic Fine. Some interlinear space must be allowed to ensure that the ascenders and descenders do not clash. So I have lettered a few lines with half a nib width and a nib width space before deciding on the latter. The depth of text will be 25 lines per page. I have chosen to range the text left. This in itself produces an inherent problem in that the right-hand margin will appear larger than the left, because of the ragged optical white space being produced. When producing the finished manuscript a minor adjustment for this will be made, by leaving more white space in the left-hand margin to compensate. In the end an extra ⅛ in (3 mm) has been added to the left-hand margin, moving the text over to the right.

Testing nib sizes for line length.

'What are moon-letters?'a

B2 nib

'What are moon-letters?'aske

italic broad nib

'What are moon-letters?'asked the Hobb

italic medium nib

'What are moon-letters?'asked the Hobbit full of

italic fine nib

'There are moon-letters here, beside the plain
runes which say "five feet high the door and
three may walk abreast".'
'What are moon-letters?'asked the Hobbit full of

italic fine nib – ½ nib width interlinear

'There are moon-letters here, beside the plain
runes which say "five feet high the door and
three may walk abreast".'
'What are moon-letters?' asked the Hobbit full of

italic fine nib – 1 nib width interlinear

'There are moon-letters here, beside the plain runes which say "five feet high the door and three may walk abreast".'

"What are moon-letters?" asked the Hobbit full of excitement. He loved maps, as I have told you before; and he also liked runes and letters and cunning handwriting, though when he wrote himself it was a bit thin and spidery.

'Moon-letters are rune-letters, but you cannot see them,' said Elrond, 'not when you look straight at them. They only can be seen when the moon shines behind them and what is more, with the more cunning sort it must be a moon of the same shape and season as the day when they were written The dwarves invented them and wrote them with silver pens, as your friends could tell you. These must have been written on a midsummer's eve in a crescent moon, a long while ago.

'What do they say?' asked Gandalf and Thorin together, a bit vexed perhaps that even Elrond should have found this out first, though really there had not been a chance before, and there would not have been another until goodness knows when.

3

ITALIC ALPHABET

Italic is a compressed style from the Renaissance period, developed by Italians from classical manuscripts of the ninth century and enjoying great popularity during the 15th and 16th centuries. It is a suitable hand for large quantities of text as it can be produced with speed and makes economical use of space.

It has an inclined angle to the right, which can vary from a few degrees to 13° from the vertical. After 13° the pen forms produced are not balanced, with straight and curved strokes differing greatly in weight.

Compression of the letterforms lessens the width differentiation between characters: the capital and lower-case 'M' are proportionally much narrower than their Roman counterparts when compared to, for example, the letter 'P'. The overall impression of italic is that of lightness and fluidity. The basic key letter in the lower case alphabet is the 'o', the left side of which is apparent in the 'a', 'c', 'd', 'e' and 'g', while the 'b' and 'p' reflect the right-hand side.

Serifs in the capitals are formed either by a change of direction of stroke, or by an upward movement before and after the main strokes. Additionally, serifs are made by overlapping curved strokes over main strokes, such as in the 'B', where the beginning of the curved stroke which forms the upper bowl overlaps the left-hand edge of the main stem. Capitals used on their own are not too successful, especially when elaborately flourished. It is therefore preferable to use plain capitals to maintain legibility when using them to emphasize a text.

Lower-case serifs are produced in a similar fashion to those of the capitals. Ascenders and descenders can be finished with an extra flourished stroke, either straightish lines curving upwards or rounded strokes ending in a slight hook or merely sheared straight terminals. They extend one nib width above the capital line and three nib widths below the x line. They can be extended beyond these areas as flourishes, but with discretion.

It will take practice before an even inclination is achieved. Build up a rhythm with a line or two of 'z', 'm', 'n' and 'o', as this will loosen up the fingers. Speed is also important in lettering, with each stroke being deliberate but not laboured. Too slow and the stroke will tremble instead of being straight.

There are two kinds of numerals which accompany the style: lining numerals and hanging numerals. The former line up with the capitals, whereas the latter vary. The 1, 2 and 0 are contained within the x height; the 3, 4, 5, 7 and 9 enter the descender area to the value of two nib widths; and the 6 and 8 are lettered to the height of the capitals.

A page of continuous text.

This layout of 'Monday's Child' is ranged left to
conform to the inclination of the lettering style
and give movement.

Monday's child is fair of face,
Tuesday's child is full of grace,
'Wednesday's child is full of woe,
Thursday's child has far to go,
to attend

calligraphy
class

Friday's child is loving and giving,
Saturday's child works hard for its living,
'But the child that is born on the
Sabbath day, Is bonny, and blithe,
and good, and gay.

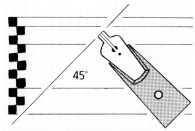

Capital height: 7 nib widths
This alphabet is lettered with a B4,
the metric equivalent being a 2·3mm.

Nib Angle approximately 45°

Arrows denote direction of stroke.
Numerals indicate order of character
construction.

Flourishing should not be at the
expense of legibility.

EGJ
KLM
PTV

W W W W X X

Y Y Y Z Z Z

Z Z & ? ? ! !

1 1 2 2 3 3 4 4

5 5 6 6 7 7

8 8 9 9 0 0

1 2 3 4 5 6 7 8 9 0

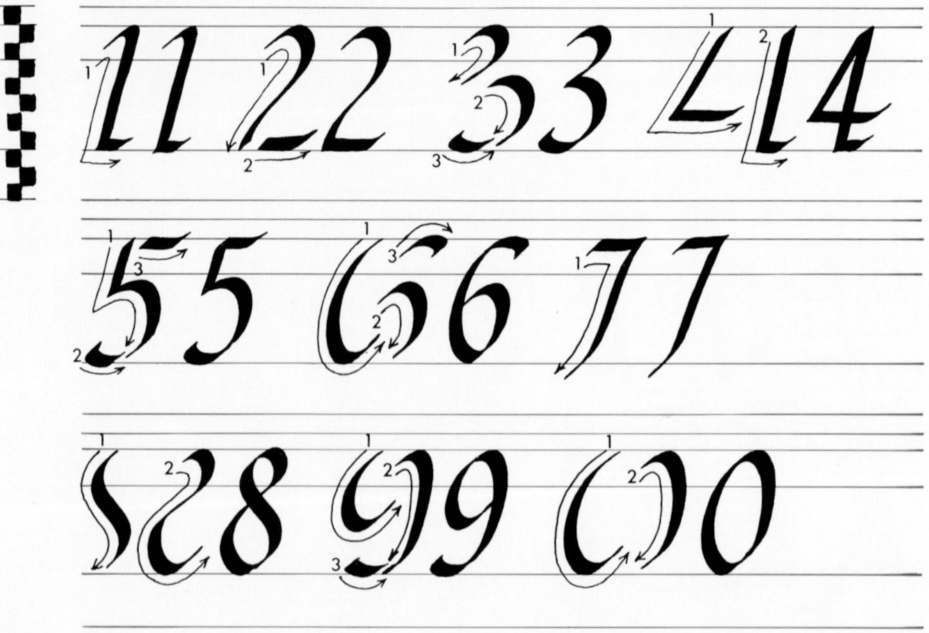

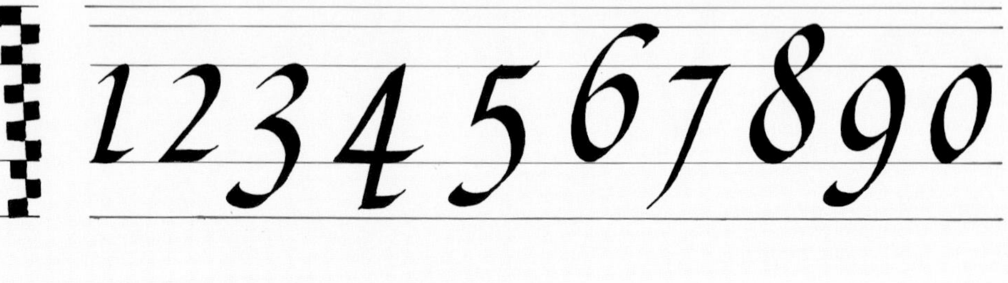

Ascenders: 3 nib widths

'x' height: 5 nib widths

Descenders: 3 nib widths

a a b b c c

d d e e f f g g

h h i i j j k k

l l m m n n o o

p p q q r r s s

t t u u v v w w

v v x x y y z z

b b d d

e e f f

g h h

p q q

r t x

FROM THUMBNAILS, THROUGH WORKING ROUGH TO FINISHED WORK

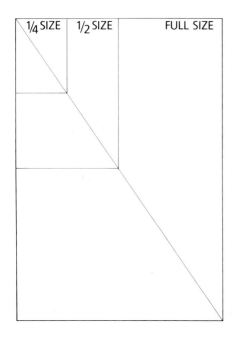

1 Jane Silvester

2 would like you to

2 come to her

birthday party

2 on 24th September

2 at 8pm Flat 3,

2 Long Lane

2 Hampstead,

2 London NW3 (RSVP)
3

Deciding on the priorities to be given to lines of text.

If the work is for an invitation card, consider its distribution. If it is to be posted, then there will be a limitation on convenient size. Unless you make the envelope yourself, you will need to know the availability of envelopes and matching paper or card. Check with a stationer which envelopes are available in small quantities to avoid having to use the same envelope and paper again and again. I have chosen a card that measures 4¼ in (105 mm) by 5⅞ in (149 mm) (or A6), which fits into a C6 envelope.

Is the invitation formal or informal? This will determine the type of layout chosen. Centred layouts are generally used for formal occasions but a ranged-left layout can be equally elegant. The use of a ranged-right layout in this instance would be unsuitable, because the work entailed in producing such a layout is too great for lettering a large number of cards. A justified layout can also be disregarded as this is used only for continuous text. An asymmetrical layout could be used for an informal card, if desired. I have decided that the copy can be treated in an informal manner and have chosen to use a ranged-left layout.

Before a rough layout can be made, it must be decided which elements should be prominent. I have underlined the words that I feel should have impact, with remaining copy being coded 1, 2 and 3 in order of importance.

Large-sized lettering, which makes up display headings, attracts the attention of the reader. Secondary information should be smaller than the display but in a size that can be read easily. Subsidiary details can be lettered smaller. The aim of the calligrapher is not only to produce a tasteful letterform but also to lead the reader through the information in a sequence that relates to the order of importance of the text.

In the sample copy, I have underlined the words 'Birthday Party', as I feel these are the key words. The person's name I have given code 1, the invitation text, time and place have code 2 and finally 'RSVP' receives code 3, as it is the least important.

The next step is to rough out some basic ideas in pencil before using pen and ink. This initial work is done on layout paper at a size scaled down from the finished invitation. In this instance half the size is adequate to become familiar with the words and to create an interesting layout by committing any initial thoughts to paper. Rough layouts should be both landscape and portrait formats to discover which shape accepts the text more readily and uses the area to its best advantage.

Begin by drawing some vertical and horizontal boxes in pencil, scaled down to represent the card. To achieve this, draw the card on a piece of layout paper and divide the rectangular box diagonally from the top left-hand corner to the bottom right-hand corner. Then divide the top line of the box into two; on my card this measures 2⅛ in (52.5 mm) to the centre line. Draw a vertical line down from this centre point to where the vertical line meets the diagonal. This is the depth of the card at half-scale. Then draw a horizontal line from the diagonal to the left-hand vertical. The area just defined is a half-size of the original card area. Naturally at a half-size, the measurements could just be divided in half and a rectangle drawn, but on a larger format, where it may be necessary to work on roughs a sixth or an eighth of the original size, this method saves time and calculations. It is also useful when scaling illustrations or drawings up or down. This is

Some initial small roughs to decide on layout.

Jane Silvester
would like you to come to her
Birthday Party
on 24th Sepember at 8pm
at Flat 3, Long Lane,
Hampstead, London NW3

R.S.V.P.

JANE SILVESTER
would like you to come to her
BIRTHDAY PARTY
on 24th September at 8pm
at Flat 3, Long Lane,
Hampstead, London NW3

R.S.V.P.

JANE SILVESTER
would like you to come
to her
Birthday Party
on 24th September at 8pm
at Flat 3, Long Lane,
Hampstead, London NW3   RSVP

Jane Silvester
would like you to come to her
Birthday Party
on 24th September at 8pm
at Flat 3, Long Lane,
Hampstead, London NW3
R.S.V.P.

JANE SILVESTER
would like you
to come to her
**BIRTHDAY
PARTY**
on 24th September
at 8pm
at Flat 3
Long Lane,
Hampstead,
London NW3
R.S.V.P.

Jane Silvester
would like you to
come to her
*Birthday
Party* on 24th
September
at 8pm
at Flat 3, Long Lane,
Hampstead,
London NW3
R.S.V.P.

Birthday Party
Jane Silvester
would like you
to come to her
Birthday Party
on 24 September
at 8pm
at Flat 3
Long Lane,
Hampstead,
London NW3
R.S.V.P.

Drawing up the card area.

Lettering 'Birthday Party' using guidelines.

discussed in more detail in the illustrations section.

Begin by using the margins discussed in the previous section, that is, one unit at the head and side margins and 1½ units at the foot. However, it is important to remember that for the roughs these margins must be half-size to keep the same proportion. It may be advisable to reduce the foot margin as the format is quite small and, provided there is more space at the foot than the head, this is quite in order. The text should be placed optically in the depth of the card. Then, using an HB pencil sharpened to a chisel edge, begin to describe the text on the rough layouts (also known as thumbnails owing to their small size).

From the rough layouts I have chosen to use the landscape format that has 'Birthday Party' lettered diagonally across the card. The angle has been fixed at the point at which the italicized letters coincide with the vertical edges of the text area. I feel that this gives stability to the layout and a reference point for the eye.

The rough now requires 'working up'. This is a term which refers to lettering out sample lines which one hopes will fit the working layout. We need to know that the rough will work at actual size before the finished card can be lettered. From the small rough, an intelligent guess can be made as to the nib sizes to use by multiplying the stroke width by two, remembering the roughs were half size. I have decided to try a B4 nib for the display lettering and an Italic Medium for the main text.

The layout is divided into three main parts, commencing with the person's name and the words of the invitation itself, then the event, and finally the venue. The main display line holds the text together and determines how large the main copy can be.

It is first necessary to draw up the card area and borders on a sheet of layout paper, but full-size this time. Start by lettering the display heading in Informal Script with the B4 on a separate piece of layout paper, having first marked out the guidelines by stepping off nib widths, then drawing in the lines with a sharp 2H pencil. Once this has been lettered it should

The words being checked against the text area for line length.

Closing up the letter spacing.

Checking that the reduced letter spaced words fit the text area.

Using a second sheet of tracing paper over the lettered text to mark off line lengths.

Beginning to letter the text.

Positioning 'Birthday Party' and marking out guidelines.

be measured against the layout, to check that the line length is correct. If it is overrunning the measure, an adjustment to letter and word spacing may avoid changing to a smaller nib.

Once the heading fits satisfactorily, the main text is then tackled. Step off the nib widths and draw in the guidelines. I have allowed a half-nib-width interlinear space in the event of descenders and ascenders clashing, and also space between the first three lines and the second three lines. After lettering the text, compare it to the layout and mark off the guidelines from the top margin for the first batch of text and from the foot margin for the second. A vertical pencil mark at the end of each line will help to gauge if lines and letters clash when the Italic line is checked against the layout.

Position the heading between the two sections of text. If it is found that there is insufficient room, use some of the extra space from the foot margin by lowering the second batch of copy. Once the position of the Italic line has been established, the guidelines should be transferred to the layout sheet.

A working layout now exists, although admittedly it consists of guidelines only. It is prudent to letter in the text by tracing over the existing lines of copy before turning to the production of the finished card. There may still be some modifications to make; after all the preliminary work it is satisfying to see the completed working layout.

The finished working layout.

Taking measurements from the working layout.

Transferring guidelines to the workpiece using a marker gauge.

On viewing the finished layout, I have decided to range the 'RSVP' to the right so that it aligns with the 'y' in 'party'. I feel this will be visually more pleasing.

The designed layout is then ready to be transferred to the chosen card, which must be slightly larger than the finished size, with a minimum of ½ in (12 mm) selvedge all round, to allow for taping the card to the drawing board. It will be trimmed off when the work is completed. The card size, margin lines and guidelines should be drawn using an HB or H pencil, being careful not to gouge tramlines into the surface – a light line is all that is required. First draw the format area, then, after stepping off the margins and guidelines on a strip of cartridge paper, transfer them to the card. The diagonal lines will have to be marked from both left- and right-hand margins.

Before beginning to letter, it is necessary to consider the colour in which the text will be written – black is hardly party-like. I have chosen peach-coloured card, with red ink for the words 'Birthday Party' and blue ink for the remaining text. A small piece of card was put to one side for trial lettering and colour checking. It is always useful to have an extra piece of the chosen material, because the action of the pen and ink may differ from surface to surface.

Position the card on the writing line, that is, the lettering position at which the student feels comfortable on the board. Tape it into position and cover with a guard sheet, leaving only the first line visible. Taking the working layout, make a fold just above the x line and position it so that the first line is just below the descender line of the first guidelines on the card. Letter the line and repeat the procedure until all the lines have been worked.

It may help to reposition the piece of work after lettering the first three lines. I personally find that it is easier to move the guard downwards for a small piece of work, where only a small deviation from the writing line is required. However, when lettering a deep column of text it is better to

Drawing guidelines on to the workpiece.

Testing various inks for colour compatibility.

Lettering out the text using a guard sheet to keep the work surface clean.

The main text completed.

Lettering in 'Birthday Party'.

leave the guard in the writing position and move the workpiece, which need not be taped to the drawing-board surface.

To letter the Italic line, the card should be turned until the text is horizontal to the writing line. The finished card should be put to one side to give the ink time to dry before removing the guidelines. This is done with a plastic eraser rather than a normal rubber eraser because it is kinder to both ink and lettering surface.

Erasing the guidelines once the ink has thoroughly dried.

Trimming the card to size, with a blade, on the waste side of the ruler.

On the stone
in letters that gave
their own light,
was a legend;
Whoso pulleth
this sword
from this stone
is rightfully

King of England

Arthur

put his hands
to the golden hilt.
The letters on the
stone blazed out;
with a metallic
hiss, the sword
slid free.

BLACK LETTER ALPHABET

Black Letter, Gothic or Old English as it is sometimes called, is a very condensed, upright style, elaborate and, in many examples, extremely difficult to read.

However, from the 10th to the 15th centuries it was the main style in use. It is difficult to imagine the reason for adopting this style in preference to Uncial or Half Uncial forms. Many believe that one of the reasons was speed, but I find this hard to accept. A style that requires five directional changes to form the lower case 'i' cannot, in my opinion, be easier to produce than its Half Uncial counterpart. I would, however, agree with another school of thought which maintains that the style was introduced as a space-saving measure. It is very economical in its use of paper because of its compactness. During the period that Black Letter was popular, there was a greater requirement for documentation and literature; so it follows that a style that required less space to convey a message would be preferred.

The style in its basic form can be regarded as vertical lines spaced the width of the stroke apart and joined together with hairline strokes. The letterspacing should be close – even to the point of touching – in order to achieve a good texture to a page.

The nib angle is 45° and at the beginning of each stroke there is a hairline serif. This is produced by moving the nib sideways at the lettering angle before changing direction to start the first thick stroke. The reverse is the case for a finishing hairline stroke. It should be noted that the direction of nib is changed three times to make the average lower-case stem with a movement towards the left, giving a slight rounding at the bottom-right side for a left-hand stroke, before finally changing direction to meet the base line.

The capitals are formed by multiple strokes. It will help students if the individual movements are traced, and the letterforms built up in this manner. This method will improve judgement of the amount of space to leave for the hairline and embellishing strokes, and assist in the accurate positioning of those strokes that join. The capitals should never be used on their own as the resulting pattern will be illegible.

Although Roman numerals were used in conjunction with Black Letter, I have included a set that I feel complement the style. There are many different examples of the form, a large proportion being fairly decorative. One of the exponents of the art was the German calligrapher and type-designer, Rudolph Koch, who produced some quite plain examples of the style while still retaining the original strength and character of the letterform. Black Letter does have a certain charm and is probably one of the few styles that is comparatively well known; it is often referred to as Old English.

The content of this passage from *The Fall of Camelot*, lettered in Black Letter, led me to the layout produced here: a centred layout creating a subtle graphic image of the hilt of the sword.

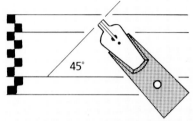

Capital height: 7 nib widths
This alphabet is lettered with a B4,
the metric equivalent being a 2·3mm.

Nib Angle approximately 45°

Arrows denote direction of stroke.
Numerals indicate order of character
construction.

Use edge of nib for vertical hairline
strokes.

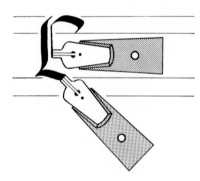

Lining numerals

Ascenders: 2 nib widths

'x' height: 5 nib widths

Descenders: 2 nib widths

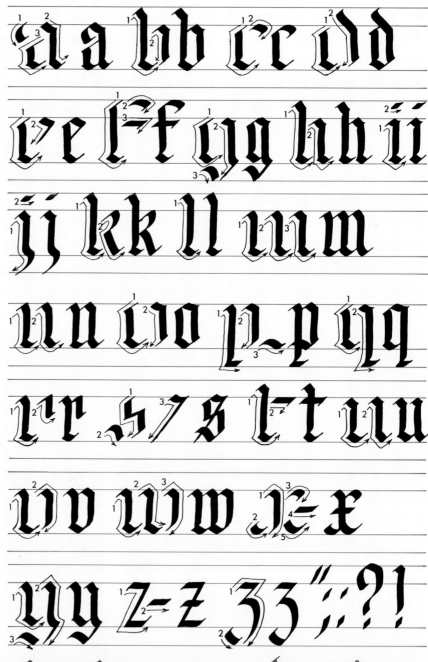

Gothic requires close letter and word spacing to produce an even texture.

VERTICAL ALIGNMENT

When ranging left, ranging right or justifying a text, consider the vertical alignment of the letterforms. Because the alphabet is made up of varying shapes – round, oblique and straight – adjustments must be made in order that one letter will appear aligned above another.

As a general rule, straight letterforms can be aligned with the margin line, while round and oblique forms will venture over the line. The capitals 'J' and 'T' will require the most movement for ranging left, as their arms project the furthest from the main stems. Practise with display sizes : large letterforms accentuate the movement involved.

The red boxes in the first four lines are ranged left. The result can be seen in the second column. Some of the words appear to be out of vertical alignment. The second four lines have been optically adjusted to compensate for individual letter shapes. The result is good vertical alignment, as in column three.

THE
FOUR
LEAF
CLOVER
THE
FOUR
LEAF
CLOVER

THE
FOUR
LEAF
CLOVER
WILL
BREAK
A FAIRY
SPELL.

THE
FOUR
LEAF
CLOVER
WILL
BREAK
A FAIRY
SPELL.

CENTRING DISPLAY LETTERING

For centring display lines, especially where a narrow measure is used, it is best to place the word within a box, which should take up the visual length of the word. As with ranged-left alignment, round and oblique or open letterforms would protrude over the edges. Take the word WELSH in the optically centred example: the 'W' will venture outside the box, whereas the 'H' will be contained. This optical width of word can now be divided in half and positioned in the layout format on the centre line. For punctuation and hyphens, space must be added until the visual line has been decided upon.

The red boxes in the first four lines indicate the true length of the word and have been centred in the second column accordingly. The second four words have been placed in boxes of optical length, the result of which can be seen in column three.

ON
WELSH
FISHER-
MEN.
ON
WELSH
FISHER-
MEN.

THE
WATER
LEAPER
PREYS
ON
WELSH
FISHER-
MEN.

THE
WATER
LEAPER
PREYS
ON
WELSH
FISHER-
MEN.

UNCIAL AND HALF-UNCIAL ALPHABET

The Uncial style was born of the necessity to create formal letterforms while achieving speed in writing. The letterforms developed after the Quadrata capitals and are true pen forms, round in character and simple in construction, being in complete contrast both to Quadrata and Rustica forms. From the fifth century they were adopted as the standard book style.

The capital letterforms are constructed between two parallel lines with a number of characters breaking through the capital and base lines, noticeably the 'D', 'P', 'G', 'H', 'K', 'L', 'P', 'Q' and 'Y'.

As with most styles variations occur in the visual appearance of certain letterforms. This is understandable when it is considered that many different scribes were needed to produce large works and a scribe, even if copying a given style, would not produce exactly the same letterform as another. This effect, multiplied over different settlements and countries, is bound to give variation in styling. Calligraphy is, after all, a projection of the letterer himself.

Half Uncial soon followed, as it was a natural progression in the search for a form that was simple to construct and therefore time-saving. In Half Uncial the breaking of capital and base lines is more pronounced, and it is at this point that our present lower-case alphabet was formed (with the exception of a few characters).

I have classed Uncial and Half Uncial as one style, the upper and lower case of the fifth to eighth centuries. For the style shown here, I have altered the pen angle from horizontal to the writing line to 20° from the writing line. Most books state that the pen angle should be horizontal but, if one considers the *Book of Kells*, it is clear that a constant nib angle could not have been used throughout the letterforms. The Book of Kells is to be found in the library of Trinity College, Dublin. It contains some excellent examples of eighth-century writing and illumination within its pages and was probably produced by the monks for use on special occasions only. In some examples the straight stems are started horizontally and are ended in the same way. However, the round letterforms have diagonal stress with oblique shading, which implies that the angle of the pen could not have been horizontal when these forms were constructed.

It is for this reason that I have chosen the 20° lettering angle. The whole of the alphabet can be lettered using only this angle, although there are some letterforms which could be improved by changing the angle. For example, in some manuscripts the diagonal stroke of the capital 'N' is almost horizontal, with just a slight dipping of the stroke to meet the right-hand vertical. This character can best be described as a Roman 'H' with a very low cross.

Be careful when positioning characters on the six guidelines. The main body of the capitals is contained within five nib widths, with the various ascender strokes being extended a further nib width. The strokes that break the base line end on either the first or second descender guideline. The main body of the lower case is within four nib widths with both the ascenders and descenders occupying two nib widths.

I have produced Arabic numerals to accompany this style, although Roman numerals would originally have been used. They are lettered to the capital height of five nib widths.

I decided to letter this piece in Uncial and Half Uncial, because I felt it reflected the Gælic origins of the Isle of Arran. The name of the island produces a repeated pattern which creates diagonal movement across the background. The choice of green was important, since it needed to be light enough for the prose, lettered in gouache, to show clearly.

"The sun ere he sunk
behind Ben Ghail,
the mountain
of the wind,
gave his grim peaks
a greeting kind,
and bade
LOCHRANZA smile"

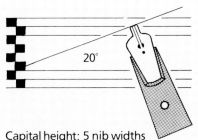

20°

Capital height: 5 nib widths
This alphabet is lettered with a B4,
the metric equivalent being a 2·3mm.

Arrows denote direction of stroke.
Numerals indicate order of character
construction.

Uncials with Half Uncial i, showing
relative positions on guide lines.

91

11 22 33

41.4 55 66

77 88 99

00 ???!

?&& "";

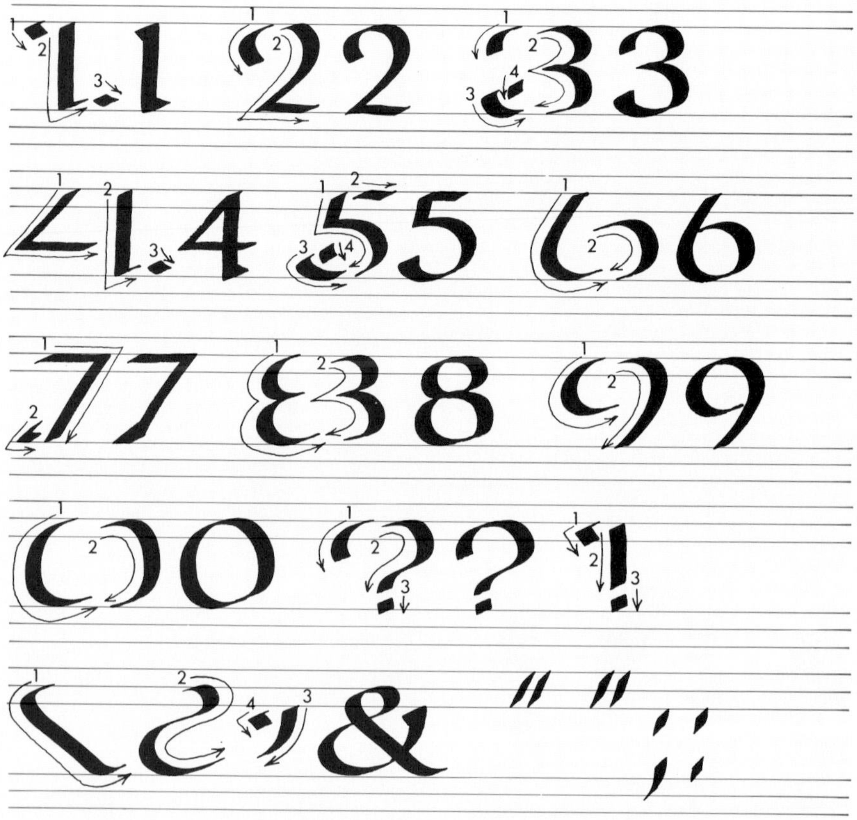

Alternative capitals

aa A A CC DD

EE F GG IH KK

MM NN TT U

WW V X y y

Ascenders: 2 nib widths

'x'height: 4 nib widths

Descenders: 2 nib widths

Alternative lowercase

CONDENSING AND EXPANDING A STYLE

The occasion may arise when the student will need to fill a given area with text. When condensing or expanding a style, always alter the letterforms on a proportional basis. If the width value of the capital 'O' is compressed by 25 per cent, then the remaining characters must follow suit, with the obvious exception of 'I', which has no room for movement.

Angles change when letterforms are condensed or expanded, and therefore the width of diagonal strokes alter accordingly. However, the main characteristics of the style should be maintained wherever possible. Letters with diagonal strokes, such as 'M', 'N' and 'W', appear very heavy if over-condensed, making words look spotty.

The standard Neo Classic style has been condensed and expanded. In each case individual letterforms have been treated similarly.

EXTRA CONDENSED

CONDENSED

STANDARD

EXPANDED

INFORMAL SCRIPT ALPHABET

In this example the word 'neon' suggested the style used: lettering in gouache on Ingres paper with nib and holder. The lay lines of the paper run diagonally across the sheet to conform to the angle of lettering. This piece of work was produced for pleasure only and as an exercise in freehand underscoring.

This informal italic – another style based on printers' type – is both modern and yet reflects earlier 20th-century scripts. The characters are lettered at approximately 13° from the vertical. This inclination works well with the 30° pen angle. The letterforms can be said to reflect constructivism (a kind of forced uniformity) in as much as certain characters follow each other in their terminal endings and flourished strokes. For example, the flourish to the capital 'B' is reflected in the 'D', 'F', 'I', 'J', 'K', 'T', 'U', 'V', 'W', 'X', 'Y' and 'Z', with mirror images appearing in the 'C', 'E' and 'L'. Likewise the loop of the 'A' appears in other characters. Needless to say the capitals should not be used on their own. As with Black Letter, they become illegible. Individuality within an alphabet makes for good character recognition. Although this is lacking in this style, I think it has its uses when displayed in a capital and lower-case form. Some alternative terminals for the capitals have been included. I prefer these as they are more in keeping with the lower-case letterforms.

When lettering the lower case it is advisable to work out the letter combinations before committing pen to paper. The reason for this is that some of the joining strokes may need leaving out in order to achieve even letter spacing.

Informal Script has a small x height with extended ascenders and descenders and is therefore unsatisfactory for continuous text but ideally suited for decorative work, where an unusual style is called for.

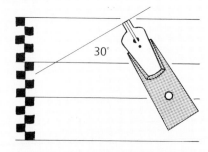

Capital height: 9 nib widths
This alphabet is lettered with a B4,
the metric equivalent being a 2·3mm.

Nib Angle approximately 30°

Arrows denote direction of stroke.
Numerals indicate order of character
construction.

The characters are inclined at
approximately 13° from the vertical.

Alternative terminals

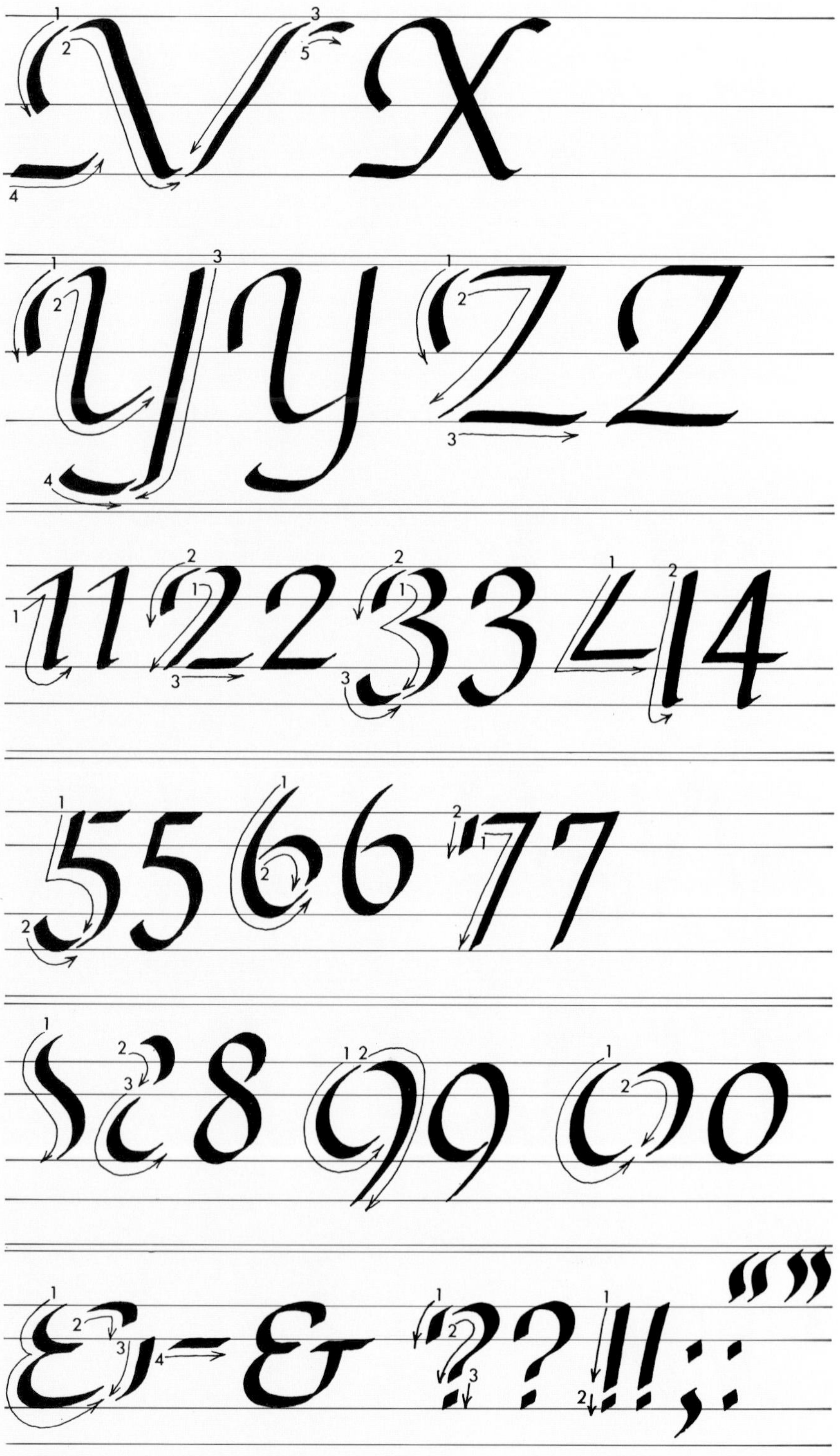

X

V V X

Y Y Z Z

11 22 33 4|4

Hanging numerals

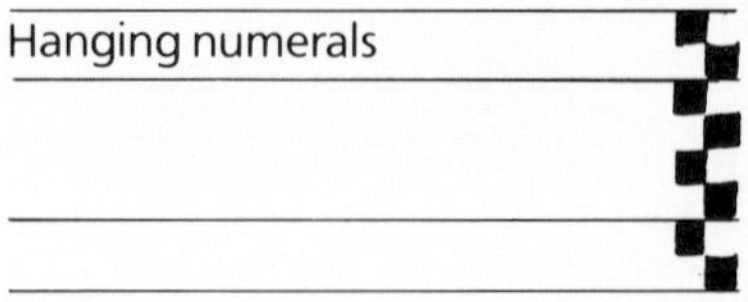

55 66 77

&8 99 00

&-& ??!!;:""

98

Ascenders: 5 nib widths

'x'height: 4 nib widths

Descenders: 5 nib widths

aa bb cc
cd ee εε
ff ff gg
hh ii jj kk
ll mm nn
oo pp qq

q q r r s s

s s t t u u

v v w w

x x y y

z z z z

Letters to be joined

THE CENTRED LAYOUT

The centred layout has an air of authority; it makes the work look official and precise. In order to illustrate the processes involved in producing such a layout, I have chosen a subject which is invariably displayed in a symmetrical format – the certificate.

Calligraphers are often asked to produce certificates for various organizations. Such requests can be of a one-off nature – a long-service certificate for example – or more commonly a series, when the awards for one major event are divided into sections and then sub-divided into first, second and third placings etc. This type of certificate can be extremely complicated to lay out: because of the many copy changes, it can be difficult to obtain an overall style which is echoed in each certificate. The copy is made up from both static and variable information.

Again, ask that all important question: what is the function of the piece of work? It is, in this example, as an accolade for achievement, for winning first place in a wine-tasting competition, and the certificate will probably be framed and displayed on a living room wall.

The size of the certificate is $9\frac{1}{2}$ in (240 mm) by $7\frac{1}{8}$ in (183 mm) and I feel that the text area should allow generous margins all round. I have settled on $1\frac{1}{2}$ units for the head and sides with 2 units at the foot. This gives $1\frac{1}{16}$ in (27 mm) and $1\frac{7}{16}$ in (36 mm) respectively (one unit being based on one tenth of the width), with a text area of $6\frac{7}{8}$ in (176 mm) deep and a measure width of $5\frac{1}{8}$ in (129 mm).

The copy must then be analyzed, coded 1, 2, 3 and so on in order of importance, with any line breaks marked. The various code numbers will relate to different-sized nibs. Some pencil roughs based on the line breaks and order of importance are then sketched out. As with the invitation card, the roughs will be at either half- or third-size, just to get the feel of the words and line lengths. They need to be fairly accurate as the lettering will be used to help decide on the nib sizes required.

In a series of certificates such as these, it is necessary to use the largest amount of copy for each of the changeable areas to ensure that they will all fit into the same format. For instance, one of the other sections is just 'Aperitif Section'. It would be pointless producing a layout which allows for this one-line heading. Obviously, when the student came to the 'Medium Red Table Wine Section' it could not fit within the same area. Likewise, the longest name, Dorothy Lawrence, must be selected and the longest placing, which is 'second'.

Although the original copy supplied may have been typed out in a mixture of capitalized words and words in upper and lower case, as it was in this example, it is the function of the calligrapher to decide upon the visual balance. Those words that I feel should be in capitals have been underlined and superfluous words have been dropped.

From the roughs it is necessary to decide which one will form the basis of the working layout. The lettered stroke widths for each size need scaling up to full size and allocating accordingly. I have chosen to use the following nib sizes which relate to the codes on the copy: code 1 means a B2 nib; code 2 italic broad; code 3 italic medium; and code 4 italic fine. When using a fountain-type pen, it helps to have enough barrels to eliminate the changing of the nib.

Deciding on the priorities to be given to lines of text.

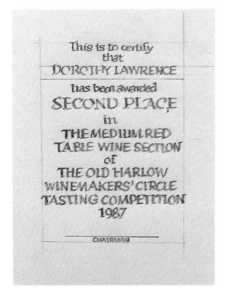

An initial thumbnail rough is produced to get a feel of the line length and copy.

A decision must be made as to which nib size to use.

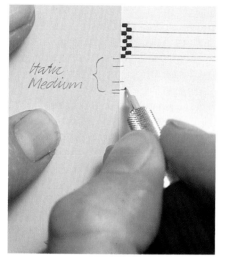

Marking out the first two lines of lettering.

Lettering.

The working layout should initially be ranged left so that the student can see if the nib sizes chosen will fit the measure. Draw up the text area, 6⅞ in (176 mm) by 5⅛ in (129 mm), on a layout sheet. Take the tightest line of the chosen rough as a starting point. Some lines will fall short of the measure and are of little concern from a fitting point. My longest line is 'Tasting Competition' and, as the test line, it must be lettered first.

On the same layout sheet as the text area, but above it, the measure requires marking, together with the guidelines for the italic broad nib. The test line must be lettered to check on the width it will make. It appears just to fit, but it will be safer to drop a nib size for the whole of the section from 'The Old Harlow' to '1987'. I feel that the layout will be overpowered by this item if it is left in its present size, but I intend to leave 'THE MEDIUM RED TABLE WINE SECTION' in the Italic Broad.

It is then possible to commence with the working layout. At this point, the depth that the text will have is unknown; so, by returning to the rough, it can be seen that it is unlikely to overrun, provided the space allocated is adhered to. Start by lettering the first two lines, allowing a nib-width of interlinear space. As the layout progresses, I will mention how to

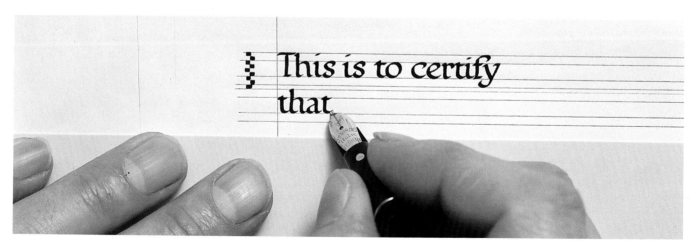

arrive at line spaces between sections of text. Note down the size of nib for each line of text as a reminder when lettering the finished certificate.

On completing the first two lines a decision has to be made as to how much space to leave between the base line of 'that' and the cap line of the name. All three lines are related phrases and, as such, should be treated similarly with interlinear space, but, as 'Dorothy Lawrence' is in a larger letterform and in capitals, the space must be optically changed to compensate for the extra area that capital letters occupy. I feel that it should be at least equivalent to the space between the base line of 'This is to certify' and the x line of 'that'. This is, of course, personal preference, and each individual will balance the elements slightly differently, but I am attempting to give guidelines and only personal experience will allow for intuitive spacing.

Once lettered, the name requires underscoring with a line. It may be that the name will be filled in after the certificates are lettered, in which case I would have to forego my preference for limiting the length of line to the extent of name and settle for the line being contained by the measure. As to the position of the line, there is nothing worse than underscored words which have a line so far beneath them as not to belong to the word. I have positioned the rule (line) two nib widths below the base line. What if the name were in upper and lower case? No problem – split the rule either side of the descender and place it closer to the base line.

Between the rule and 'has been awarded', I favour the unit of space used before, although this may need changing slightly because there are four ascending letters in the line. The spacing of the lines throughout the remaining copy will be based on this unit of space. Where there is more than one line of capitals, I intend to insert one nib width of interlinear

Deciding on a space value.

Underscoring using the edge of the nib against an inverted rule.

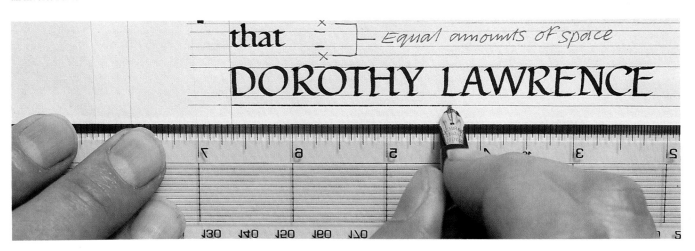

The finished working layout shows that extra space will be added where marked with an asterisk. The pencil lines at both ends of each line of text indicate the optical length necessary when centring the text.

This is to certify
that _____ Equal amounts of space
DOROTHY LAWRENCE *
has been awarded *
SECOND PLACE *
in *
THE MEDIUM RED
TABLE WINE SECTION
of *
THE OLD HARLOW *
WINEMAKERS' CIRCLE
TASTING COMPETITION
1987

CHAIRMAN CHAIRMAN

Centring by the folding and creasing method.

Marking the centre crease.

Finding the centre by measuring with a ruler.

space, using the nib being employed to letter those particular lines. Once the whole copy has been lettered and a depth arrived at, further alterations can be made if necessary.

Having reached the signature line, I prefer the word in small capitals as opposed to the Italic Fine capitals. They are drawn with the same nib but the height is limited to the x line. Small capitals can often be seen following a person's name when Honours or Degree letters are present.

The space that is left between '1987' and the rule for the signature can be halved and ample space will still be left for the signature. I intend to take half of the present space and divide it by eight with one-eighth of the space being inserted as extra interlinear space in the seven asterisk positions marked.

The working layout is almost complete. In order to centre the lines on the finished certificate, it is necessary to ascertain the centre of each line of lettering or, to be more precise, the optical centre. The end of each line should be marked as if the work were to be ranged left and right, that is, the part of the first and last letter of each line which would rest on the margin line to give vertical alignment. Show these lines in pencil on the working layout.

Once the lines are marked, the length can either be measured and then halved and marked in pencil, which is the method I favour, or, alternatively, the lines of the layout can be cut up and each line held up to the light, loosely folded until both ends of the line meet, then pinched in the centre to give a firm crease. This method is better employed where one-off pieces of work are concerned. For repeated lettering, such as certificates, I prefer my original layout to remain intact as pieces of paper have an odd way of disappearing just when they are needed most. If you do decide to use the cutting method, make sure that you have made a depth gauge for the work before slicing your finished working layout into strips.

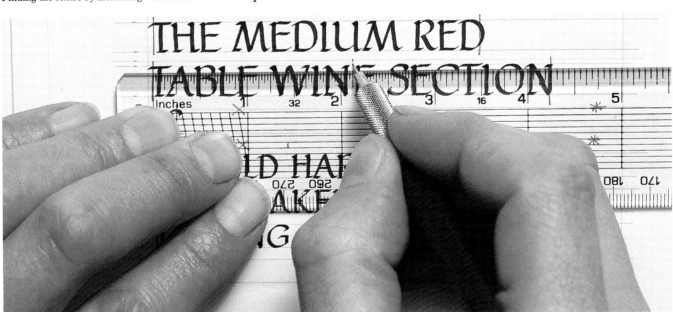

Transferring the guidelines to the finished surface.

A portion of the depth gauge used.

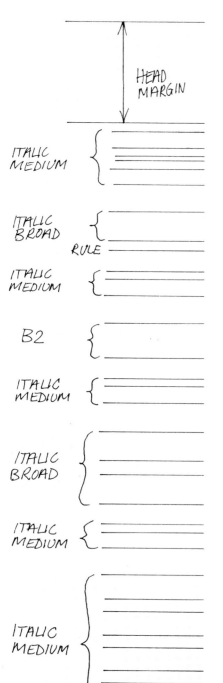

From the working layout, two gauges must be prepared: a depth gauge showing the full depth of the work, head and foot margins and each line of lettering in its correct position, together with the nib sizes and any additional information that may be required; and a width gauge showing the side margins, measure and centre line (C/L) and any other items that are felt necessary. Each time a certificate requires marking out, the process is simplified considerably by using gauges. Naturally, the system can be used for any type of work which needs the same information to be transferred repeatedly to a finished workpiece. The gauges are taped on to the drawing board in a position above and to the left of the workpiece. All the lines are transferred to the finished working surface in H or HB pencil. The sheet to be lettered must have a paper guard to prevent it from getting dirty.

Before commencing final lettering, the question of colour must be considered. I have chosen to use a sandy-coloured paper with black and red lettering after producing a small rough just to confirm which lines will appear in red. This rough has been produced with fine-tipped, water-soluble fibre pens which do not bleed (spread) on the paper. I have opted

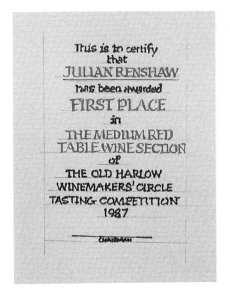

to have only the name and placing in red, because to include the section as well makes the layout bottom-heavy.

To use the working layout as a guide, fold it over so that the ascenders of the first line of text are on the creased edge. Then slip it behind the guard sheet with the centre line of the first line of text registered (positioned) with the centre line of the sheet to be lettered so that the guidelines are visible. Commence lettering with the appropriate pen at the start of the line shown on the working layout.

This process is repeated until the finished certificate is lettered; the layout sheet is folded each time and the finished work surface raised for each line to be lettered.

Once the certificate is completed, allow a little time to elapse before attempting to erase the guidelines. Many a fine piece of lettering has been ruined by students who are too anxious to see the finished product.

A small rough to show colour.

Lettering the finished certificate.

This is to certify
that

JULIAN RENSHAW

has been awarded

FIRST PLACE

in

THE MEDIUM RED
TABLE WINE SECTION

of

THE OLD HARLOW
WINEMAKERS' CIRCLE
TASTING COMPETITION
1987

CHAIRMAN

NEO CLASSIC ALPHABET

Based on printers' type and converted for the pen, this style, with its small x height and extended ascenders and descenders, has a quality that appeals to me. The letterforms break many of the traditional rules of Roman construction, but the high cross-bars on the 'E', 'F' and 'H' and the disproportionate upper bowl of the 'B' add to its character. The serifs are formed by secondary strokes to the main stems. The lower thinning curve to the capital 'C' and 'G' and the lower-case 'c' and 'e' are given an additional stroke to give the terminal some body.

The nib angle is 30° with only a few minor adjustments. The capital 'K' has a change to the nib angle for the thin diagonal stroke, being lettered at 15° to the horizontal to give the stroke some weight. The capital 'X' and 'Y' have the same adjustment as the 'K', and the capital and lower-case 'Z' both have the pen angle changed to horizontal to give bulk to the main diagonal stems.

The lower-case 'a' is unusual because it breaks another rule regarding the nib. The upper thin stroke of the bowl is lettered against the nib, very lightly, to give it body before it changes direction to form the thick stroke of the bowl. The stroke could be thickened by second stroking in an upward direction to meet the main stem, which would eliminate working against the nib.

This style can be used for display purposes on posters, leaflets and handbills, but I feel that it is ideal for an invitation or something similar.

This verse from the song, 'A trick of the tail', developed into a strange layout in which the elements are ranged left and right and centred within the design.

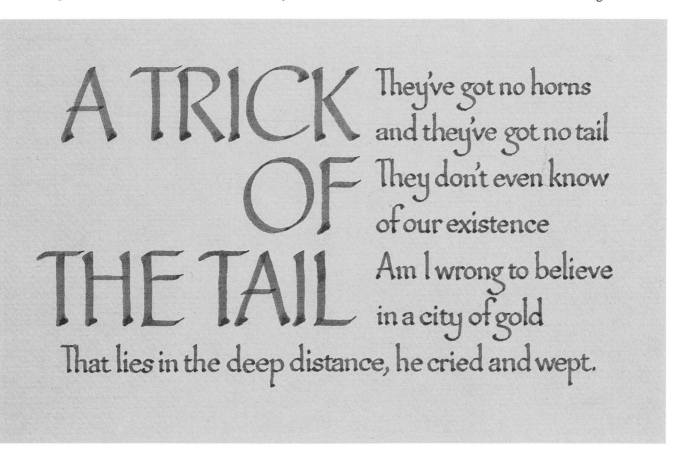

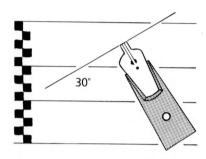

30°

Capital height: 9 nib widths
This alphabet is lettered with a B4,
the metric equivalent being a 2·3mm.

Nib Angle approximately 30°

Arrows denote direction of stroke.
Numerals indicate order of character
construction.

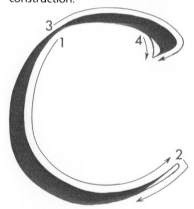

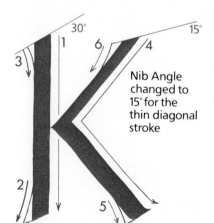

Nib Angle
changed to
15° for the
thin diagonal
stroke

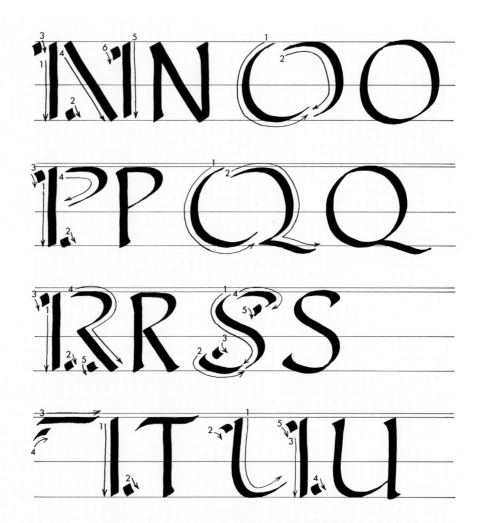

Nib Angle changed to 15° for the thin diagonal stroke

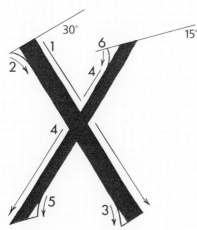

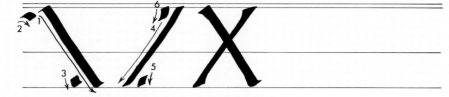

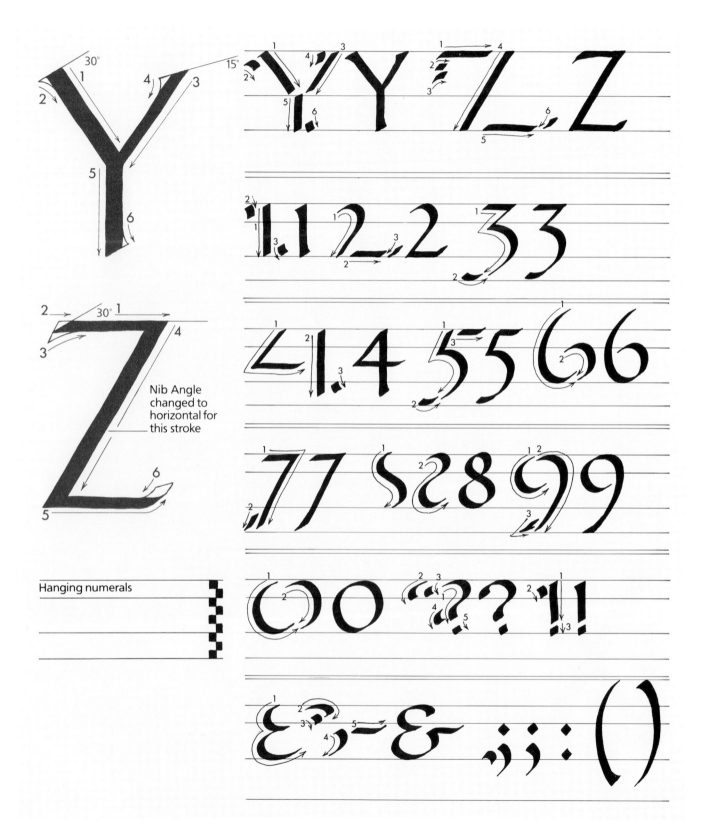

Nib Angle changed to horizontal for this stroke

Hanging numerals

112

Ascenders: 5 nib widths

'x' height: 4 nib widths

Descenders: 5 nib widths

r r s s t t

l l u v v w w

x x y y

z z

Some flourished letterforms

G

A E K L

Q R S

CALLIGRAPHY AND ILLUSTRATIONS

When combining illustration with calligraphy, it is important to create harmony between both elements. The illustration should reflect the square-edged pen, as do many early manuscripts, with line drawings making full use of the implement and the varied stroke widths it will produce. Textures can be built up by cross hatching (strokes in opposing directions) or by moving the pen angle from a thin stroke gradually through to a thick stroke position and vice-versa, giving a vignetted (gentle graduation of) line weight.

There is no easy way to learn how to draw with a square nib, and if, like myself, the student does not regard himself as an illustrator the only way to succeed is by involvement and practice. I have spent many years analyzing woodcuts, and they have given me inspiration for various projects as they adapt well to the pen. Thomas Bewick produced some of the finest woodcuts known and turned wood-engraving into an art form.

I would suggest, when considering illustrative work, that the student obtain photographic or printed references before commencing. Once he has an idea of the image he wishes to accompany a piece of calligraphy, he should search his own or a local library for suitable images or photographs, books and pamphlets. Searching for material will heighten the student's awareness of the images he sees every day. I store away illustrative references like gold dust, with any image I feel that may be remotely useful tagged in books or magazines for future use. A scrapbook of likely subject matter is a wonderful idea and takes very little time to add to each week. References should be as detailed as possible so that new images can readily and accurately be created from them.

I learnt my lesson some years ago when employed by a leading auction house. I was asked to produce a poster for a sale which included prints of bicycles. The print chosen for the image of the poster was slightly soiled and faded and depicted a man riding a penny farthing. I duly produced a drawing for the printers, but when the posters arrived I realized, to my horror, that the front wheel of my penny farthing would never have

Tracing the image to be used from illustrative reference.

Shading over the underside of the tracing.

Tracing the image on to the finished surface.

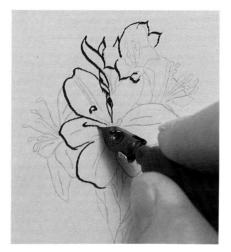
Inking in the initial outline.

The finished illustration.

turned because of my positioning of the front pedal. Very early days in my career, and a mistake which fortunately only I had noticed. With more adequate reference it could have been avoided, but it taught me to check carefully the images I create.

Once the necessary references have been found, the student will need to transfer them to tracing paper. If the size of the illustration required is the same as that of the reference material, it can be traced directly on to the

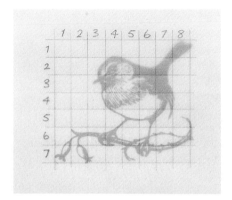

Confining the illustration to a gridded square on tracing paper.

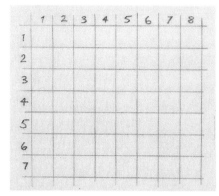

Drawing a gridded square to the required enlargement.

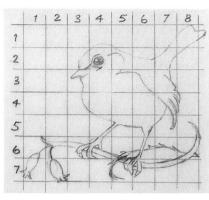

Plotting the image on the grid.

Building up the illustration.

Shading over the underside of the tracing.

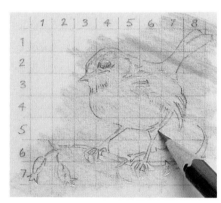

Tracing the image on to the finished surface.

Traced image on finished surface.

Inking in the initial outline.

The finished illustration.

tracing paper, using a 2H or H pencil (or lead in a technical pencil). Take care to interpret the image exactly, because what is produced on the tracing sheet will be the image traced down on to the finished piece of work. Once the tracing is completed, the sheet must be turned over and the underside of the drawing area shaded over with an HB pencil. Turn the tracing paper over again so that the image side faces upwards and position it on the finished surface of the work using masking tape at the

The Jolly Miller

There was a jolly miller once,
Lived on the river Dee;
He worked and sang
from morn till night,
No lark more blithe
than he.
And this the burden
of his song
Forever used to be,
I care for nobody, no!
not I,
If nobody cares for me.

Some designs which I have used for bookmarks and Christmas cards.

On the first
day of
Christmas
my true love
sent to me.
A partridge
in a pear
tree.

117

head (top) to hold it gently in place. Then trace the drawing down by going over the lines of the image using a hard, sharp pencil, 2H or 4H. When completed, lift the tracing sheet, without unfastening, to make sure that the drawing has been successfully transferred to the finished surface. The faint image must now be inked in with a fine, square-ended nib. Build up the image slowly, referring to the original reference for the finer points.

Should the reference material found not be the correct size for the design, then it will be necessary either to enlarge or reduce the image. First contain the illustration within a square or rectangle on a sheet of tracing paper, subdividing this by small grid squares. The size required should then be drawn as a square or rectangle on another sheet and subdivided as before. Number the squares horizontally and vertically on both sheets of paper and plot your image from the reference material to the correctly-sized grid.

Signs of the zodiac. Some have been taken from English and German woodcuts and adapted for the pen. The Crab, Scorpion and Scales are my additions, as the originals were not suitable to be contained within a circle. The shading in the lower portion was necessary to give a uniformity to the twelve symbols.

CLASSIC ROMAN ALPHABET

This style has been included as an alternative to the traditional Roman form, Quadrata, which is an extremely difficult letterform to produce with a pen. To form the serifs requires many strokes using just the edge of the pen. However, with this Classical Roman alphabet, the serifs have been simplified for ease of lettering with the pen; so it may not be a true classic Roman but will pass as a pen-rendered version. Here the serifs are either formed at the end of a curved stroke by slightly hooking the pen or by a completely separate stroke, lettered at a shallower angle than that of the main stroke construction.

The letterforms are made with a pen angle of 30°, with a few exceptions. The vertical strokes of the capital 'N' are lettered at a nib angle of 45°. This steeper angle means that the vertical strokes will appear narrower, and the contrast of weight is more in keeping with other letters in the alphabet. The diagonal strokes of both the capital and lower-case 'z' also have an adjustment to them. Here the main stroke is lettered with the pen angle parallel to the horizontal, giving the main stem more body.

The horizontal serifs are lettered at a pen angle of 20°, which gives a reasonable proportion with the thin strokes in the alphabet. The serifs on the upper main stem of the 'B', 'P' and 'R' are extensions of the thin cross-strokes which form the upper bowls of each letter. Where white areas are left between serifs and main or thin strokes, they should be filled in afterwards.

The accompanying numerals are lining numerals, lettered to the capital height. Hanging numerals may, however, be used, should the occasion arise.

When lettering in Classic Roman, a simple, centred layout is often all that is needed. The letters speak for themselves.

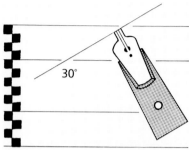

Capital height: 10 nib widths
This alphabet is lettered with a B4,
the metric equivalent being a 2·3mm.

Nib Angle approximately 30°

Arrows denote direction of stroke.
Numerals indicate order of character
construction.

Final filling in must be done where spaces occur between serif and stroke.

Nib Angle changed to horizontal for this stroke

Lining numerals

Ascenders: 4 nib widths

'x' height: 6 nib widths

Descenders: 4 nib widths

123

30°

Nib Angle changed to horizontal for this stroke

30°

RULES AND BORDERS

Decorative elements have been used to complement letterforms for almost as long as the written word has existed. Early manuscripts display decorative initials so elaborate in form as to lose the legibility of the character being embellished. Common sense and restraint must prevail and decorative enhancement play only a secondary role to that of communication. All a student's efforts therefore should be directed towards maintaining legibility while retaining harmony between text and illustrative work. I feel this is of paramount importance if the work is to be functional as opposed to just clever or fashionable.

Before applying decoration to a piece of calligraphy, question its relevance. Does the text require embellishing? There may be good reasons for adding a border, tailpiece, swelled rule, box rule, cartouche or similar device. Short rules are often introduced as divisions between sections of text, on menus for instance. Tailpieces are regularly seen as ornamentation at the beginning or ending of chapters; and box rules or borders assist in emphasising sections of text. They all have their applications, but over-indulgence can result in the original message being overpowered by fanciful imagery.

When combining calligraphy with rules and borders, spare a thought for the compatibility between the letterform and the ornamentation. As letter styles have their place in periods of history, so too does decoration. Black Letter text with a 1920s or 1930s border would not be appropriate.

If asked to produce work that requires the use of borders, search a central library under the printing section. Sufficient reference will be found there not only for samples of 'flowers', 'arabesques', 'rules' and 'borders' (these are primarily printing terms), but also for the appropriate period to which they belong.

Alternatively the student can design his own borders. Do not be put off by thinking they are too complicated, as most borders, once analyzed, can be easily reproduced, since they are based on the repetition of basic designs. For example, a simple border can be designed around a 'flower' (the decorative unit) and be contained within a square measuring seven nib widths by seven nib widths. This could be subdivided to give reference points for the beginning and ending of the various elements within the flower. This border may also require a 45° corner device, as it is

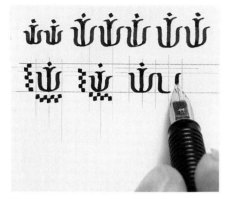
Deciding on the proportions of the flower.

Designing the corner device.

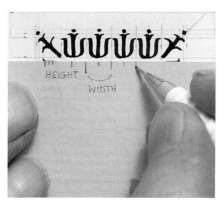
Transferring the unit values to a strip of card.

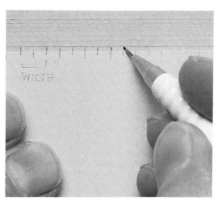
Transferring the values from the card to the finished surface.

The finished border used as an 'Ex Libris' for a friend's library.

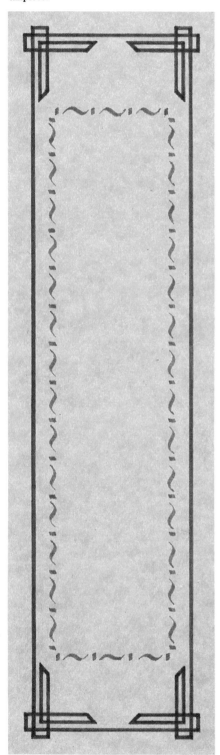

Useful decorative items for the calligrapher: some borders, a cartouche, swelled rules and a tailpiece.

not symmetrical, and possibly the foot of the flower might face inwards on each side of the border. The size of the border is established by multiplying the width and depth of the decorative unit respectively.

For the cartouche and the tailpiece in a large border, preliminary work is carried out on tracing paper. Only a half or quarter of the image requires developing as the repetition is achieved by inverting or mirror-imaging the original drawing when tracing down on the finished surface.

INDEX